Top 18 Proven Strategies

for a Successful Career

in Real Estate...in Any Market!

Top 18 Proven Strategies
for a Successful Career
in Real Estate...in Any Market!

Including Bonus Tips, Templates, and Samples

Dianne Dunn
REALTOR®, Broker, CRS, GRI

The Silloway Press

Columbia, MD

Top 18 Proven Strategies for a
Successful Career in Real Estate…in Any Market!

Printed in the United States of America
    LCCN: 2010940971
    ISBN-13: 978-0-9826293-5-2
    ISBN-10: 0-9826293-5-3

Copies of this book and all forms and templates may be purchased at www.SuccessfulRealEstateTips.com.

The Silloway Press, 9437 Clocktower Lane, Columbia, MD 21046
301-335-9368 – Top18@SillowayPress.com - http://SillowayPress.com

This book is dedicated to Heather L. Dunn,
my loving daughter and best friend.

Acknowledgments

Throughout the years, there have been so many people who have encouraged and inspired me, both with my career and with writing this book, and it's with the most sincere gratitude that I thank them.

Over the last ten years, one of the most endearing and supportive groups has been the CyberStars™, where I've met many new friends who have willingly and graciously shared their ideas and systems. Many thanks to them, and foremost to Allen F. Hainge, the founder of this wonderful group.

A special thank you to my Keller Williams colleague and friend, Donna Harmatuk, who has been a great friend, partner and source of continued support; to Maggie Crosby-LeBlanc, our KW manager and friend, whose heart and soul are always there for support; and to Mike Tavener and John Prescott, who were so instrumental in helping us get started with the New Bern, NC, Keller Williams Office in 2005.

I'm also grateful to my Realtor® friend Marvin Bullock, who presented me with a book a few years ago about writing a book, and strongly encouraged me to share my years of experiences in this business. I laughed when he would email me real estate questions, addressing them to "Master" and signing them with "Grasshopper."

Thanks to my former neighbor and friend John Hoarty who patiently helped me with and my website and technology, before websites were the in thing to do.

There are so many friends, both in Northern Virginia and North Carolina, who have inspired my success and perhaps don't even know it. Cheers to my dear friends Janice Esser and Karen Swanson, who in the early years had supported and encouraged me with goals like completing my Broker classes in 1980. At the time, I was raising a two-year-old, actively pursuing my real estate career, and feeling like I had too much on my plate; I was definitely ready to drop out of class. Thank you for helping me find the perseverance to hang in!

Also, I would like to thank John Hoofnagle, my first broker/manager in Reston, Virginia, who took three weeks of his time to train a rookie agent in the early days of 1976 when organized training was not the norm in the real estate industry as it is today.

Many thanks to my parents, Dan and Sue Fredericks, whom I trust are looking down from their resting place and hopefully are proud of the achievements and strides I have made during my life. Pop taught me that you can get through most any challenge in life with patience and a little humor! To my four younger sisters, Pat Fredericks in Arizona, Susan Navarro, Barbara Nicolis and Michele Corcoran in New York, who have looked up to me as their big sister. While we're separated by distance, they're always there providing love, support and fun.

A special thank you to my publisher, Peg Silloway, who patiently walked me through the process of my first book.

And most importantly, from the bottom of my heart, a sincere thank you to my husband Lee and daughter Heather, who have formed the core of my life, and who have given me the encouragement to write this book.

Contents

Preface

Did you know that the custom of giving tips in the service industry is thought to have started in the 17th century? "To tip" meant simply "to give." Restaurants had boxes labeled with T.I.P. (To Insure Promptness) on the wall beside their entrances. Patrons who wanted their food served quickly placed a few coins into the box before they sat down at their tables.

While there are many ways of conducting your real estate business, today I want to share with you my tips. These are not hypothetical ideas or suggestions written by motivational speakers or authors. Rather, they are my real-life experiences — the ideas, the mindset, and the systems and tools that have served me well over the years to help build a successful real estate business and career.

I have asked myself, "What are you doing writing a book? You are not an author!"

What I am, however, is a real estate professional with 34 years of full-time experience, with a focus on the residential side of the industry.

After some cogitating, the answer that came to me was simple: I have a passion for the real estate business and love to share! While I have enjoyed working with thousands of buyers and sellers throughout the years, I have also enjoyed mentoring and teaching classes to agents. Some of these classes were organized courses designed by different real estate franchises I was affiliated with where I had to become certified to teach. Others were my own personal creations including power point presentations with step-by-step clear visuals and examples on how to complete and perfect a specific task or undertaking. Many of these training visuals also included some of my favorite quotes and a little humor, since I feel that a good laugh every now and then eases the tension when we are dealing with very important real estate transactions.

I've also learned through my experiences that when I placed customer service as my Number 1 focus, then business followed and referrals flowed. If clients feel that money is your main focus, then they become a one-time only sale without the rewards of future business.

Whether you're a seasoned agent or new to this business, I hope that my successes and challenges will help you grow. Real estate is all about people and developing trusting relationships. When you add knowledge, good systems and effective tools that you develop and master, then you're on your way to a successful career!

I've been honored and humbled over the years to win numerous multi-million dollar awards,

REALTOR® of the Year awards, and other special awards and accreditations. (After all this time, I think I have enough plaques to wallpaper a room!) I have also had the opportunity to manage and mentor a wide range of real estate agents drawn from two companies throughout my career. I feel now, that it's time to "Give Forward."

If you don't have a real passion for this business and are not motivated and willing to dedicate your time and efforts to succeed, then you should probably put this book down now, and consider another job or career. If, on the other hand, you truly want a successful, long-term career in real estate, then read on with me!

Seth Godin, successful author of *The Dip*, *The Big Moo*, and "Seth's Blog," said, "A true gift is a heartfelt connection, something that changes both the giver and the recipient."

This book is my heartfelt gift to you that will, hopefully, change or improve your life in real estate!

The forms and templates in this book are samples; full size versions are available for purchase online in editable MS Word and MS Excel formats at:
www.SuccessfulRealEstateTips.com

1

Dinosaur or Sage?

My life before real estate

Prior to real estate, I held a position in the marketing department of IBM and worked with many sales people and customers — first in New York, then in Northeast Pennsylvania, and finally in Washington DC. I believed that excellence was considered the standard to strive for, and I learned from this company that people were rewarded for dedication, self-discipline and hard work. I was proud to be part of a successful company, which also rewarded me.

Ten years later, it was my husband who was instrumental in my decision to leave the big corporation and get my real estate license. In his view as an attorney, real estate law was the most fascinating part of law school, and he encouraged me to jump to a new career. It was a difficult leap, but I made it.

As I look back now, it certainly was comfortable having a guaranteed salary, benefits, and a retirement fund! I had no idea what was in store for me; however, I would not trade the experiences, challenges and fun of being an independent contractor in real estate for anything!

Does 34 years make me a dinosaur or a sage?

My real estate career has now spanned many years and, like some of you, I've been through several real estate recessions and boom markets. My experiences have shown me that the key to surviving is focus, dedication to service, and a positive attitude. Dinosaurs became extinct, but if people think outside of the box, expand their knowledge, and embrace technology, they don't need to follow them on that route. It's an ever-changing industry: Just because my first introduction to keyboarding was on a manual typewriter, that doesn't mean that I can't develop proficiency with today's computers and technology: it just takes a commitment and effort.

> *"Technology won't replace agents. Agents who know how to maximize technology will replace agents." — Burke Smith*

Challenging markets

In the early 1980s' recession, the prime rate was 21 percent, conventional rates for home mortgages were 18 percent, and lot loans were dried up. At that time, some conventional loans were assumable, and the VA (Veterans Administration) and FHA (Federal Housing Administration) loans were fully assumable by anyone, without qualification. (Quite different from the market of 2010!)

The challenge then was that most buyers did not have the full amount of cash to assume these loans. Lenders introduced new loans called "wrap-around" mortgages, for which buyers still had to qualify with certain ratios. However, they could put down as little as 5 or 10 percent on an existing 8 percent VA/FHA assumable loan, and the lender would wrap the old loan into a new mortgage for 12 percent. Though 8 percent and 12 percent interest rates in today's market sounds astronomical, back then buyers were delighted to have those lower rates!

The second scenario I'll never forget was a beautiful home listing I had in 1982 which in a "normal" market would have sold within 30 to 60 days. After nine months on the market and a lot of hard work, we finally received an offer from a buyer who really wanted to purchase this house. However, in order for the buyer to qualify for the loan, which was 16.5 percent at the time, the loan had to be bought down to 14.5 percent with points paid to the lender (every 1 point = 1 percent of the loan amount, and a buy-down meant that it took 1 point to bring the loan amount down for every 1/8th percent). At that time most lenders were quoting 14 to 16 points or more to handle the transaction! Fortunately, one of my trusted lenders agreed to take the loan for 6 points total, which after days of negotiating, the buyer and seller ended up splitting.

Can you imagine scenarios like that in today's market? Yet, we were able to get the house sold, and everyone was happy!

I mention these examples above, since I hear so many agents complain today about how tough the real estate market is. While I can empathize with their concerns, my point here is to show that there are challenges in any market. If we are committed to this business and we persevere, we can make it through any market with success.

2

Ethics and Practices

Make it a win-win

R eal Estate is a competitive business, but that does not necessarily mean that you cannot have a professional, win-win relationship with your peers. A win-win is where every party to the transaction achieves their main goal, considering the current conditions of the market.

Buyers and Sellers can be in an emotional state when they are in negotiations for the purchase or sale of a home. That's to be expected since home purchases or sales are one of the largest investments they make.

Agents, on the other hand, need to be calm and think objectively. We have the knowledge and experience to offer suggestions which will help all parties come to an acceptable agreement. We need to expand our horizons outside of the box of our individual marketplaces for new ideas and experiences which we can adapt to our own market.

I have enjoyed meeting and sharing ideas with numerous agents, both in my marketplace and all over the country. These exchanges and sharing of information help us grow.

I enjoy reading and perusing some of the daily and weekly real estate e-newsletters. There's so much information on what's happening around the country that will affect our industry. Remember, in the residential real estate industry, what starts in the west, generally moves east! There are numerous published articles by successful agents from which we can glean a point or two on what will work in our own marketplace.

The difference between a Realtor® and a real estate agent

There is a difference between a real estate agent who is not a member of NAR® and a Realtor® who is. You can be one without being the other. That is, all licensed real estate agents are not Realtors®, but all Realtors® are licensed real estate agents. Both must pass their state's licensing exam. In addition, however, a Realtor® must join the National Association of Realtors® (NAR) and takes a pledge to be bound by NAR's Code of Ethics. By joining the NAR, a Realtor® also becomes a member of their state and local association.

Unfortunately, we all meet some Realtors® who are blindly competitive, perhaps to the point of undermining other agents or being outright unethical. Whether this type of behavior is considered tricks-of-their-trade, or they honestly don't know any better, it certainly is a shock when you first experience one of them.

Often, these Agents/Realtors® will be reprimanded for either ethics violations by their local board/association, or by the state's Real Estate Commission for blatantly violating a section of the real estate law.

Agents/Realtors® who are reprimanded are in jeopardy of losing their licenses for 30 days, 60 days, or even permanently. Aside from the economic impact, should you be charged with a violation, there is the time-consuming and gut-wrenching cost in preparing your defense and presenting it to your state's Real Estate Commission. Therefore, be sure that you conduct your business in a professional manner.

On a lighter note, but certainly with sincerity, one of my former brokers, Stewart Smith, encouraged everyone to conduct themselves in an ethical and professional manner so that, in his humorous words, we would stay out of "Real Estate Jail!" While there really is no real estate jail, his caution with using this term made it very effective!

Code of Ethics

Become familiar with our National Association of Realtors® (NAR) Code of Ethics, which we have all sworn to abide by when we join the NAR. Copies of the Code can be found on NAR's website www. Realtor.org.

Our duties are specifically presented in 17 Articles and Standards of Practices. The Articles are divided into three different sections:

◆ Duties to clients and customers
◆ Duties to the public
◆ Duties to other Realtors®

The Code of Ethics has gone through extensive changes, and new guidelines are issued each year, based on the changes or challenges in our industry. For instance, Internet marketing and advertising did not exist several years ago. However, several Standards of Practice were finally introduced in 2007 and 2008, specifically describing how Realtors® should present a true picture in their Internet marketing, advertising and the use of domain names.

TAKE ACTION!
Review the NAR® Code of Ethics on www.Realtor.org.
1. Duties to Clients and Customers
2. Duties to the Public
3. Duties to Realtors®

It's All in a Word or Name

Threatening or comfortable?

Can you identify with some words that may have a different effect on people? For example, a friend of mine works as a manager for a national insurance investigation firm where they hire investigators to research claims. The investigators have been advised to introduce themselves as "field administrators" rather than "investigators," since that word seems very threatening to many people.

Consider the term *agent*. While we are all licensed real estate agents, that word might be too closely associated with FBI agent or CIA agent, which might indicate secrecy or even be a little too threatening to people. Based on what we do (or should be doing), a better term would be Real Estate Consultant. A consultant is a much better term for what we do and the effect that it has on people might be a softer touch. We "consult" with them on their needs, preferences, and dreams before we begin the process of helping them find the home of their choice. You might want to consider your next order of business cards with the title Real Estate Consultant after your name.

Professional and trusting?

There is one word in the real estate industry that, for me, portrays the feeling of a quick-flip for money and/or a challenge to professional integrity, and that is the word *deal*. Rather, the more appropriate term should be a *real estate transaction* which means carefully following the process of the sale from beginning to closing to ensure a smooth transaction for buyers or sellers. Remember, in this business, it's all about people trusting us to guide them in the right direction towards their ultimate goal.

Another very familiar term in our industry (that is often mispronounced) is *Realtor®*. Being a Realtor® means that, in addition to passing your state exam and getting your real estate license, you have joined the National Association of REALTORS® (NAR), in addition to your state and local associations or boards. It means that you have taken the required Code of Ethics courses, and are bound to follow the 17 Articles and Standards of Practice of the National Association of Realtors®. The word is pronounced Real´-tor — two syllables, with the emphasis on the first one. This word is so often mispronounced that the National Association has dedicated an entire chapter on their website to its correct pronunciation. Remember, we are professional Real-tors.

Explain the acronyms

A word about acronyms: All too often in this business, we tend to "talk" real estate terms, such as ESIK (eating space in kitchen) or FROG (finished room over garage) — and the public has no idea what we are talking about. It's fine to talk among ourselves this way, but we need to be careful when we are in conversations with prospective buyers and sellers and use the real (or lay) terms so everyone understands what is being discussed.

> **TAKE ACTION!**
> Think about what you say before you speak.

How Much Money Will I Make?

The 80/20 Rule

If you want to get an idea of your income, apply the 80/20 Rule. What does this mean? In the late 1800s, an Italian economist named Vilfredo Pareto discovered a principle that has had an enormous impact on economics and business ever since. He said that you could divide members of society into the "vital few," the 20 percent of the population who controlled 80 percent of the wealth, and the "trivial many," who possessed only 20 percent of the wealth. This is known as the "Pareto Principle."

- The Pareto Principle or 80/20 Rule, states that 20 percent of your activities will account for 80 percent of your results in any business. Consequently, we should focus on our 20 percent, so that we can reap 80 percent of the benefits.

◆ Some real estate surveys now report that
the 80/20 Rule is becoming the 90/10 Rule,
where 90 percent of all real estate transactions are done by only 10 percent of the
agents, and the remaining 10 percent is
shared by the other 90 percent, who are
most likely part-timers or those who dabble
in this business.

Don't be a dabbler! Today's true real estate
professionals are Real Estate Consultants. These are
the agents who have voluntarily taken their time
to acquire the knowledge and training to provide
superior service to the clients, and understand their
responsibilities. They guide and help their clients,
and understand the challenges of relocating.

The true Real Estate Consultant also realizes that
the purchase of a client's residence may be one of the
largest investments that their clients will make in a
lifetime. The Consultant deals with clients seriously
and provides exceptional service. The Real Estate
Consultant also understands that future referral business from satisfied clients is the key to success, and
can be very rewarding and fun! That's the secret to the
money they make.

How did I lose that listing?

Unfortunately, this question is asked too frequently by some real estate agents. How many times
have you seen a new listing come out in your MLS

(Multiple Listing Service), only to discover that it was a property that you had previously sold to these sellers. You're puzzled and shocked: "Why did they list with that agent? They were my clients four years ago when they purchased the property, and now, they never called me back to represent them in the sale!"

The big question is, what did you do, or NOT do, that led them to list their property with another agent? Did you keep in touch with them with regular mailings, emails, personal notes, and phone calls, etc? Did you let them know that you are still in this business and want to be their Real Estate Consultant?

How do buyers and sellers find their new Real Estate Consultant? Perhaps they get a personal referral from a neighbor who worked with an agent who stayed in touch and provided excellent service. Perhaps they regularly receive a monthly information newsletter from another agent, who has been focusing on their neighborhood for new business.

There is a term called "TOMA," for "Top of Mind Awareness." (Zan Monroe, CRS instructor, author, and national speaker, uses this term in his seminars.) If we follow the TOMA guideline and keep in touch with our past clients, then hopefully they will return to us with repeat business. If we don't stay in their minds, then these clients may forget our names very quickly.

My keep-in-touch program

My experience has taught me to keep an updated, very special list of clients...my past clients. Here's a sampling of what they receive from me throughout the year, every year:

- A thank you gift at closing
- A thank you letter about two weeks after the closing
- A monthly e-newsletter showing local statistics on the current market
- A magnetic calendar showing the dates of national and state sporting events, whether it's football, baseball, or golf tournament
- A magnetic calendar for the new year, mailed out in early November, with a holiday greeting
- An anniversary card for the date of their home purchase, including a couple of pages of personalized return-address labels
- Another fun monthly e-newsletter based on the celebrations for each month, e.g. Happy New Year, Valentines Day, St. Patrick's Day, Easter/Passover, Mother's Day, etc. Each newsletter contains tips on the history of the event, as well as links they can go to for recipes and fun things to do for kids. The original creation of this newsletter was done by Alice Held, a CyberStar™ friend of mine from Phoenix, Arizona. I requested Alice's

permission to use some of the materials and changed it into a format for my clients and prospects. People love receiving these types of items, and many send me thank you notes for keeping them on my mailing list.

◆ My annual Free Thanksgiving Pie Event (the brainchild of Leslie McDonnell, a CyberStar™ friend in Chicago, IL) for which I personally invite past clients to stop by the office two days before Thanksgiving to pick up a delicious homemade pie from one of our local bakeries. They love it, and it's a great way to see them face-to-face again. Not only that, but they come to me!

◆ During January, I send a nice letter to clients who have purchased and sold through us that year, along with a copy of their signed HUD closing statement, which they will need for tax time.

If we think of service — outstanding service to our clients — as our main responsibility, then the repeat business, referral business, and the money will follow!

TAKE ACTION!

1. Make a list of all the activities you do as a real estate professional...then categorize them in two columns: 80 percent and 20 percent. The tasks in your 20 percent column should be the ones that make you productive and that only YOU can do. The remainder can be delegated.

2. Make another list of ways or things that you can do to communicate (touch base with) on a regular basis with your past clients, and the people you know.

Appearance is Everything!

Dress code

We've all heard the cliché that states "You can't judge a book by its cover." In this industry, that may be true when you see a prospective buyer who is dressed in blue jeans, driving an old car and is looking at expensive homes. This may well be the buyer who can actually afford the property, as opposed to the one who drives up in a fancy car and wearing designer clothes — only to discover later that their poor credit rating prevents them from purchasing the expensive home that they feel they deserve.

However, in most cases as a real estate professional, appearances are extremely important. How comfortable would you feel if you had a scheduled appointment with your doctor, attorney, or CPA and discovered them in shorts and a tank-top when you walked into their office? It would make me feel that I wasn't important enough for them to dress professionally.

The same holds true with real estate agents. I'm not suggesting that everyone dress in suits every day, as was expected years ago when I worked in a larger metropolitan city. Times have changed, and much of our entire society is now a little more casual. However, it is important to dress one notch above the norm for your area; you will command more respect from those you meet and work with.

For example, if you work in a beach resort area, it might be more comfortable for your buyers if you dress more casually, but not if you're in shorts and flip-flops. Just like a house showing…you only get ONE chance to make a good first impression, so make sure that yours is a professional yet approachable one.

Your car

It's not necessary to drive the latest, most expensive car or vehicle. What is important is that your vehicle be clean and comfortable. By comfortable, I don't mean heated leather seats; rather, I'm speaking of a four-door vehicle that is easy for your clients to get in and out of. Imagine working with an older retired couple with some health issues; you don't want to have to use a step-ladder to help them get into your truck or SUV.

Similar to how you dress, you want your vehicle to be in line with your marketplace. If you are concentrating on first-time buyers, then your shiny new Maserati might suggest that you are already wealthy and might not have time to spend with them.

Your manners

In general, our industry does not always have the best reputation. Why? Maybe it's because there are still too many real estate licensees looking for the quick buck and who have no desire to treat the business as a long-term career. Therefore, many consumers have had unsatisfactory experiences with some real estate agents.

Therefore, we need to act like professionals. In addition to our appearance:

- We need to be prepared for each appointment.
- We need to be on time for each appointment.
- We need to avoid foul or "off-color" language with our customers and clients.
- We need to listen carefully after asking a question and not interrupt clients with our thoughts, so we can understand their needs and what their real priorities are.
- We need to be prompt with returning phone calls.
- We need to communicate on a regular basis to keep the buyer or seller updated on their transaction or search.

While some agents might say that these focuses on appearance are trivial, remember that our objective here is to stand out above the crowd and gain the professional respect of buyers and sellers.

> **TAKE ACTION!**
>
> 1. Check your wardrobe: Do you have enough professional clothes to wear when you meet prospective clients? If not, buy a few new items, or check out the local Goodwill stores — they have some great selections at very reasonable prices.
> 2. Clean your car (inside and out).
> 3. Make a commitment to be on time for appointments, and schedule a regular time to return phone messages.

Do You Have a PMA?

To be a successful real estate agent, you need to have a Positive Mental Attitude (PMA.)

Did you ever wake up feeling great and enthusiastic, looking forward to another beautiful day, only to find that when you got to the office, you heard agents moaning, groaning, and complaining about the lack of business? You think, "Oh, no, I don't want to ruin a great day!" This is exactly the time when you need to jump-start your PMA and avoid the doomsday group! After all, in our business, people want to listen to and work with honest and spirited people. By spirited, I mean people who smile often and try to make the house-hunting experience one that is rewarding, pleasant, and fun for them.

How our PMA can affect other people

Did you ever notice that when you step into an elevator with other people, most of them step back against the wall, generally keep their heads down, and do not say a word. However, if after entering the elevator, you smile and say "good morning" with an enthusiastic attitude, it's amazing how many people suddenly smile and respond pleasantly back to you. You might even discover that this produces more conversation.

How can you acquire a PMA?

- Surround yourself with other positive-thinking people. It's amazing how just being around other positive people can change your thinking.
- Avoid hanging out with the negative ones: they will wear you down!
- Read motivational books on new approaches and positive thinking.
- Sign up for a seminar conducted by a good motivational speaker.
- Sign up for a webinar, also by a good motivational speaker.

According to the Mayo Clinic, the advantages of positive thinking for your health include:

- Increased life span
- Lower rates of depression
- Lower levels of stress
- Greater resistance to the common cold
- Better psychological and physical well-being

- Reduced risk of death from cardiovascular disease
- Better coping skills during hardships and times of stress

All this suggests that a PMA is very beneficial to us not only for our business and personal lives, but also for our health, so begin each day with a positive mental attitude, and you'll be surprised at how many people will be attracted to you.

TAKE ACTION!
1. Resolve to wake each day with a smile and move forward with a positive attitude.
2. Purchase at least one motivational book on positive attitudes — and read it.

The Key Roles of an Agent

Real estate agents really have roles in three key areas that need to be mastered in order to be successful: *Marketing*, *Sales*, and *Customer Service*. Many of us are not experts in all of these areas and may want or need help in one or two of them. Help can come from many sources:

1. Your broker or other experienced agents in your office.
2. Professional training courses in which you learn how to master these roles yourself.
   AND/OR
3. Other professionals who you hire to handle specific tasks in these roles. While this may require an additional up-front cost for you, it will save you money and time in the end.

Marketing

There are two key goals to marketing yourself:

1. First, you want to brand yourself so that your name becomes a familiar term for those who are seeking real estate services.
2. Second, you want to expose the home or property that you are listing to the highest number of potential buyers.

Are you creative and "tech-savvy" with ideas and tools so you can market yourself easily, as well as the property? If you're not, it's OK; these tasks can be delegated, but they are still your responsibility to get them done.

Sales

This is an important step: It involves providing the reasons why you selected specific properties for your clients, and why it's important for them to choose one. Confidence is a key element here. While confidence will come with experience and practice, there is a way to gain confidence more quickly, and that's through research and education.

◆ Study your marketplace; know the statistics of the closed sales so you can compare them with properties that are currently available for sale. Know and understand your Multiple Listing Service and the information and charts that it can provide for you.

- ◆ Develop sales scripts that are non-threatening to the client and comfortable for you.
- ◆ Practice these scripts with other agents or in front of a mirror until you feel confident in what you are saying.

A sale starts with a decision-making process by the client. All clients love to have choices, whether they are buyers or sellers. So provide all the information you can so that they can make the best choice. And, don't forget to ask if they're ready to put their first choice on paper!

Customer service

As previously mentioned, customer service is critical to earning repeat and referral business. Outstanding service means following up on details and giving your customers and clients attention so that they know that they are an important part of your business. It's all about going that extra mile.

It's easier to provide outstanding service when you are only working with one or two clients. However, as your business grows, you will find that it can be mentally and physically exhausting to provide the kind of outstanding service that you want to give each one of them. When it reaches that point, then it's time to delegate some regular follow-up tasks to an assistant or virtual assistant. (We'll talk more about delegating and hiring assistants in Chapter 17.) This will save you time for the face-to-face or phone conversations with your clients.

TAKE ACTION!

1. Develop a "brand" or logo that you like, and implement it on all your correspondence.
2. Research your MLS and study your marketplace so that you know your local statistics. Put them down in writing and update them monthly.
3. Develop and practice scripts that are comfortable for you for communicating with prospective clients.

– 8 –

Organization and
Time Mangement

Focus, dedication, and patience

Make every minute count; make a commitment to yourself that you will learn at least one new thing every day.

According to Webster's dictionary, focus is "the point where rays of light, heat, etc. come together" — that is, where you concentrate on a clear image. That clear image in real estate is the big goal that you set for yourself. Each one of our goals and aspirations is different, so there is no one standard to follow. Focus on what you want to achieve, and don't worry about what your peers are doing!

Webster's describes dedication as "to set apart for, or devote to"; this is where you set aside time to work toward a specific goal, which in this case is your professional real estate career. It is extremely rewarding to finalize a closing with buyers or sellers who are pleased with your services and who express their gratitude. Many of my past clients have sent thank you notes, and some have even sent me flowers and gifts. I'm humbled by this, and love the personal satisfaction that this gives me, knowing that I've helped someone achieve their dream.

These successes don't happen overnight, however, and that's where you need patience. Webster defines this as "the art of enduring pain, trouble, etc. without complaining, and calmly tolerating delays."

Focus is crucial to goals and time-management, as are dedication and patience. They are guides that keep us on track, and allow us to keep our business moving forward, while having a "personal life" outside of real estate.

Get organized

After you have your mindset in a positive direction and your plan is to work on lead generation, you need to get organized. While some of us might be able to work proficiently with 6 inches of paperwork hiding our desk top, most of us work better in a well-organized office space.

- ◆ A good database management system. Whether you are using paper files or an electronic database management system, get those set up first. A few real estate database management systems include:

◇ TopProducer®
◇ AgentOffice®
◇ ACT!

My database system (TopProducer® 8i®) allows me to schedule recurring events, such as company meetings, local board meetings, and functions, etc. I simply add the task, and a couple of clicks to repeat that task, whether it's weekly or monthly. I can even have the system send email reminders of an upcoming deadline for a newsletter or article that I'm committed to write.

A good database management system also offers "Action Plans" which can be assigned to each transaction or individual leads. These are a series of follow-up tasks including phone calls, automatic emails of information, and mailed copies of pertinent information which are completed on a specific date. Action plans can be set up for different types of business, such as:

◇ Action Plan for new business leads
◇ Action Plan for new listings
◇ Action Plan for buyer closings
◇ Action Plan for seller closings
◇ Action Plan for follow up after closing

These action plans can be set up as automatic reminders to you or your assistant for the date when a task should be completed. Most database systems offer standardized letters and emails which can be edited and customized with your information, logo and letterhead. There's also a place for adding notes on each case or person. These types of systems make it very easy to keep track of all customers, clients and transactions, rather than shifting through paper notes in files.

In addition, my system also synchronizes with my smart phone (a phone that connects with the Internet and my email) so that I have my entire calendar and information on listings and closings in hand at all times, especially when I'm on the road. (Samples of Action Plans can be found at the end of Chapter 15)

◆ Review your calendar every morning and evening so you will know what you need to plan or adjust for the day ahead. You can review it by day, week or month. I prefer to set my electronic calendar screen by week, so I can review the week at a glance, and see if I need to juggle some tasks or appointments.

◆ Create a list of all the people you know for "lead generation." Challenge yourself to make a specific number of calls each day. Document the highlights in your database system, and set up a follow-up reminder to touch base with them again on a regular basis.

◆ Business cards: Make sure you have a good supply, and keep them handy with you at all times. Place some in your car, your office and your home office.

◆ If your company has an agent directory of phone numbers, keep a copy in your car, as well as at your company office and your home office, so that it's easily available.

◆ Keep a list of your active listings and pending closings readily available (with contact names and phone numbers). If you are using an electronic database system, then this will synchronize with your smart phone. If you don't use an electronic database system, then keep a paper copy with you at all times so you can refer to dates and times.

◆ Make sure you have the necessary office supplies — extra batteries for equipment, an extra supply of ink cartridges for your printer, etc. There's nothing worse that starting a project and realizing that you need to stop and purchase a basic.

Start with a plan

I know, I know: everything we read and hear about having to do with goals tells us to "write them down." While we may tire of hearing that over and over again, it really is true.

When I see a written checklist of things to do, it helps me to focus on getting them completed. Try starting with a five-year goal (which is really your dream), then a one-year goal, and then monthly goals. After you have the monthly goals set, then it's easy to break them down further into weekly and daily tasks to obtain those objectives. Plus, it's also extremely satisfying to check off those items as completed, rather than having to constantly worry about them.

Time management

Time management is the ability and self-discipline to stay on-track with a schedule you have created for your business and your free time. It is critical if you want a healthy life, along with a successful real estate career.

Five time-wasting foes

There are five insidious time wasters that can derail you from following your goal:

- Busy work: Doing trivial, minor, or unnecessary tasks. Ask yourself, "Will these tasks pay off, or would I be better off delegating them?"
- Procrastination: This is a result of a dislike of the task or insufficient interest in the task. Sometimes, it's also the fear of failure.

◆ Disorganization: This could take the form of driving back and forth between the same places, rather than organizing one convenient route to handle your errands and tasks, or of having files for one property in several different places.
◆ Excuses: The solution is to Do it, Delegate it, or Forget it.
◆ Regrets: As Ralph Waldo Emerson said, "Finish each day and be done with it."

Good time management simply means that you set aside time on your calendar, each day, week, month, or year, to focus on the particular tasks that are important to you. For example:

◆ You might set aside the first hour of each day reviewing your MLS "hot sheet" (that's where the new listings and pending and closed sales are listed, and it's very important that you are up-to-date on the current market). I'm a morning-person, so this is my 6:00-7:00 a.m. task.
◆ Set aside one to two hours of lead-generating time each day. This is when you contact the sphere of people who know you and who are in the position to refer business to you.
◆ Set aside some time to return phone calls from the previous evening and to respond

to email inquiries. Ideally, you'll be at your computer with a good database management system, and you'll have the notes that are relevant to each case and call.

◆ Block out time in the mid-morning or afternoons for appointments with prospective buyers and sellers.

When I was new to the business, a colleague was exasperated with appointments scheduled at 5:00 or 6:00 p.m., the time that she wanted to be home preparing dinner for her family. She noticed that I generally left the office before 5:00 p.m. and asked me why I wasn't plagued with that schedule. My answer was that I gave the buyer or seller options that fit comfortably into my schedule. I would say, "Is 7:00 p.m. comfortable for you, or would 9:00 a.m. tomorrow morning work better?" It's all in how we educate the public and take control of our time.

Many times throughout my career, I've had the opportunity to work with agents who feel that they are very successful because they have the numbers and statistics to show for it. However, many of them are so busy and scattered in different directions that they don't feel that they have time to breathe. If you ask them about their goals, plans, or time management systems, they most likely will say "Oh, I'm too busy for that kind of stuff." They basically live for real estate

24/7; they are workaholics, and many struggle with their personal life.

It's easy to identify this type; simply look for these traits:

- The agent feels the need to answer the cell phone immediately, rather than wait to listen to the message back at their office, where they can provide a better response after checking on the details of the case. They allow their cell phone to constantly interrupt them, thereby interrupting the current task at hand — and risking offending the person they are with.

- The agent who rushes out of the office to meet a prospective buyer at a property before finding out anything about them. Are these prospects serious buyers? Are they qualified buyers, or are they just looking for a free tour guide? There's also a possible safety issue for the agent in handling showings in this manner.

- The agent who rarely attends company meetings or a class. They might come for the beginning, but rarely stay through the end. They usually leave early to check messages and emails for fear that they will miss something. Consequently, they never receive the full benefit of the material that is presented.

- ◆ The agent who answers their phone at home during dinner time or other quality family time.

These are examples of the old-fashioned way of doing business — the 24/7 agent who feels the need to be "on-call" at all times or risk losing business. They don't realize that they must respect their own time first; when they do so, their clients will also respect their time.

I'm not suggesting that you don't answer your phone if you're in the middle of serious contract negotiations that may have a deadline. We all know that happens from time to time, but that's not the norm.

Several years ago, I was corresponding with a buyer who was coming to look at our area in two weeks and wanted to see some properties on Saturday and Sunday. They felt that two days was sufficient time, since they were also looking at other areas along the East coast.

I politely answered that I would be delighted to show them our city and some properties; however, I was not available on Sundays, since that was my day off with my family.

Interestingly enough, when they emailed back, they apologized, saying they understood how important time off and family were and that they could change their plans to Friday and Saturday, if that was convenient for me!

That's what I call time management. If you respect your time, then so will others.

Think about it: How many business people, whether they're attorneys, doctors, CPAs, electricians, plumbers, etc., can you reach by phone at 8:00 or 9:00 p.m.? Most of the time, you hear a voicemail requesting you to leave your name, number, nature of your call, and information on when your call will be returned (during regular business hours).

Set your goals

Gary Keller, the founder of Keller Williams Realty, has a system in his book, *The Millionaire Real Estate Agent*, called the "4.1.1: 4 weeks, 1 month, 1 year." Write down your goals (personal and business) at the beginning of each year, and then break them down to months and weeks. Since our business is generally in a state of "change," you will need to revise and update these goals and tasks on a quarterly or even monthly basis. If you follow a practice like this, then you are on your way to meeting your goals through a good time-management system!

Goals can be established for personal and family time, as well as for business. Examples of goals might be:

◆ Business:
  ◇ Amount of money I want to earn over the course of the next year.

◇ Decide on the best education course I can take that will help me improve my real estate skills this year.
◆ Personal:
◇ Improve my health with more exercise and better eating habits.
◇ Determine how much personal time I need each week — and then take it.
◆ Family:
◇ Attend sports games and participate in my children's school and social events.
◇ Take a summer and/or winter vacation with my family.

What goals do you have for yourself? Deciding on them will help you establish your personal time-management chart (see the sample goal chart, below).

TAKE ACTION!
1. Organize your desk, calendar, filing system, etc.
2. Set up a real estate database management program.
3. Draft your goals on the template provided.
4. Review and edit them until you feel that you have a comfortable (but challenging) set of goals.

My Action Goal Worksheet

Name: _____   **Month/Yr:** _____

My Business Yearly Goals

- ☐ 1.
- ☐ 2.
- ☐ 3.
- ☐ 4.
- ☐ 5.
- ☐ 6.
- ☐ 7.
- ☐ 8.
- ☐ 9.

My Personal Yearly Goals

- ☐ 1.
- ☐ 2.
- ☐ 3.
- ☐ 4.

My Business Monthly Goals

- ☐ 1.
- ☐ 2.
- ☐ 3.
- ☐ 4.
- ☐ 5.
- ☐ 6.
- ☐ 7.
- ☐ 8.
- ☐ 9.

My Personal Monthly Goals

- ☐ 1.
- ☐ 2.
- ☐ 3.
- ☐ 4.

My Business Weekly Goals

Week 1:
- ☐ 1.
- ☐ 2.
- ☐ 3.
- ☐ 4.

Week 2:
- ☐ 1.
- ☐ 2.
- ☐ 3.
- ☐ 4.

Week 3:
- ☐ 1.
- ☐ 2.
- ☐ 3.
- ☐ 4.

Week 3:
- ☐ 1.
- ☐ 2.
- ☐ 3.
- ☐ 4.

My Personal Weekly Goals

Week 1:
- ☐ 1.
- ☐ 2.
- ☐ 3.
- ☐ 4.

Week 2:
- ☐ 1.
- ☐ 2.
- ☐ 3.
- ☐ 4.

Week 3:
- ☐ 1.
- ☐ 2.
- ☐ 3.
- ☐ 4.

Week 3:
- ☐ 1.
- ☐ 2.
- ☐ 3.
- ☐ 4.

Education and Training

Knowledge is power, whether it's the knowledge of knowing your specific marketing area or the knowledge of how to work with specific situations like foreclosures and short sales during recessionary times. Whether you are a new agent or have been in this business for several years, learning new real estate principles and updating your skills should be a never-ending process, since there are so many changes happening in our industry. I cannot stress enough how vitally important education is, so it is vital that you dedicate yourself to continuous learning.

At a minimum, all state real estate boards have mandatory update classes, or continuing education requirements that each agent must take to keep their license active. However, these requirements are not always enough for you to excel and thrive in a challenging market. What more can you do to improve your skills?

Attend voluntary classes

To be really successful, you must be on the cutting edge of all real estate knowledge. This means investing a certain amount of time and money to take courses and classes to improve your knowledge and the systems of your business. You want to be in that 10 percent of all real estate agents who do 90 percent of the business.

Sometimes, it may mean travel if these courses are not offered in your area. When that happens, select a course that is located in a place where you would like to go. Perhaps you want to take a vacation; why not combine the course and your time off at the place of your choice? Or perhaps you have family or friends you would like to visit. Find a course or class in those areas. As an added bonus, for income tax purposes, you may be able to deduct a portion of the trip that is attributable to the real estate class.

If you're with a company that offers regular training classes, then sign up and take advantage of them. Always bring a notebook to any class or meeting that you attend. Jot down the key highlights that you want to remember, and review them later. I'm amazed by how many agents do not bring a note-taking device to meetings or classes.

If your company does not offer regular training classes, then check your local board office or your state's association website to see where classes are being held. Most states offer NAR® professional designation courses, in addition to classes by some excellent national speakers. Take advantage of them, and "invest" in your future business knowledge.

Through the years, I have taken classes which have greatly improved my skills. Here's a sampling of courses you might want to consider:

- Graduate of the Real Estate Institute, GRI®. This is a three-week course, broken down in one-week sessions. I recall that my first session in the early 1980s started with about 200 agents. Over the course of the next six months when the second session was held, there were about 100 agents, and during the final class, we had about 60 in attendance. You see, it's easy to start anything, but it takes commitment and perseverance to finish! Today, the GRI courses are offered in many more locations — class sizes are much smaller, and I feel that's more of a benefit to the student.
- Council of Residential Specialists, CRS®. When I finished the requirements in 1987, this course consisted of three different two-day sessions, held at different times, along with documentation of a specific number of closings that had already been completed. Today's sessions are grouped into one five-day session where you can complete the entire course in one week.

- Broker. Some states require that all agents become full brokers through extensive continuing education, while some states allow agents to remain as associate brokers, working under the supervision of a Broker. I invested time for the additional required courses at that time and received my broker's license in 1981.

- Accredited Buyer Representative, ABR®. A two-day course focusing on all the responsibilities of representing a buyer under a written agreement.

- Accredited Staging Professional, ASP™. This was a two-day course that I took in 2007, as our market was tumbling. Staging a home can be nearly as important as pricing when you're in a buyer's market, with a high inventory of homes to choose from. The course was held in a city about two hours away, and I was the first in my area to take the course and receive the accreditation.

- Certified Internet Professional, e-PRO®. This designation is obtained through a series of online study courses and is held by less than one percent of all agents. Its aim is to increase your proficiency with email communication and using the Internet.

- A course on Going Green, taught by a CRS instructor in 2007, provided valuable information for agents to share with buyers, sellers, and builders, on how to save on energy while protecting our environment.

There are many other certification courses, which some agents jokingly call the "alphabet soup" (referring to the letters listed after an agent's name). Whether it's alphabet soup or not, a tremendous amount of knowledge can be obtained through taking these voluntary courses and their updates.

One other thing to remember about the acronyms of these certifications is that the general public has no idea what they mean. So, a good idea is to identify these with a brief explanation, either on your bio sheet or on the back of your business card.

Listen to audio training programs

Many top national authors, instructors, and coaches have audio programs. Pop the CD in your car and listen to them while you're on the road. Make every minute count; make a commitment to yourself that you will learn at least one new thing every day.

Attend webinars

On-line webinars are the classrooms of the future. There are so many offered in which you can receive all the information online, in the convenience of your own office or home. Some are free of charge, and some have a registration fee. Remember that you are investing both your time and your money in your future career.

The local MLS (Multiple Listing Service) in our area started offering webinars on different improvements to our system, and I found them extremely helpful.

> → *TIP: Purchase a headset with a USB port that connects directly into your computer; that way, you don't need to rely on your phone line. It's much easier, and the volume is very clear.*

Sign up for free e-newsletters

There are several weekly or daily email newsletters that are free and filled with numerous articles relating to our business. I'll pour my coffee in the morning and peruse these newsletters to find ideas and suggestions. A few of my favorite online newsletters are:

- RISMedia.com — "Today's Real Estate Advisor"
- BrokerAgentNewsletter.com
- RealtyTimes.com

There are also some fee-based email newsletters that are worth subscribing to. Remember, these types of expenses are an investment in your future. One good example would be Inman News. This publication is emailed on a daily basis, and contains current topics as they relate to the real estate industry. The fee is somewhere in the $150/year range, and well worth the money.

Find a mentor

Check with your Broker first to see if your company has an established mentoring program. Some agents might be open to the concept of mentoring, and be very flattered that you admire their skills and success. If you don't ask, you'll never know.

Listen and learn from those successful and ethical Realtors® around you whom you would like to emulate. Ask if you can accompany them on a listing or buyer appointment, or attend a closing with them.

Since most successful agents are very busy, you might want to consider offering some compensation for their time. Let's say they spend time with you on different appointments, answer all your questions, or help you with your first listing appointment. In exchange, you might offer them a nominal referral fee on your first three closings. That's certainly a win-win situation for both parties. You receive the guidance and knowledge from the seasoned agent, and they receive some compensation for their time.

Hire a coach

Over the past few years, many successful agents have signed on with professional coaches to provide accountability and help them grow their business to even higher levels. Professional coaches are generally paid by the hour or flat fee. Most will ask you to sign a contract with them, since they too, are running their own independent company.

The benefit to having a coach is the regular meetings or phone calls by another person to help keep you on track with your goals.

TAKE ACTION!
1. Sign up for some free real estate newsletters.
2. Sign up for one good webinar.
3. Review the education classes offered in your area, and sign up for one of them.

– 10 –

Where Do I Find Buyers and Sellers?

The biggest challenge for most new Realtors®
is "How do I get started?" On the other hand,
the biggest challenge for some seasoned Realtors® is
"Where did all my business go?" Obviously, the real
estate business has its series of ups and downs. That's
why you need the focus, dedication, and patience to be
consistent, so that you can succeed in any market.

Somewhere in my training, I discovered a picture
of a pipeline with two open ends. If you keep feeding
one end of the pipeline with new leads, then the business keeps flowing out of the other end in the form
of closings. If you stop feeding the pipeline, then the
flow of closings on the other end eventually stops. It's
really that simple.

Leads

Closings = $$$

While company "floor time" and open houses can help you get started, it's up to you to keep generating leads for new business. (More on open houses later in this chapter.)

Lead-generation

We keep hearing that term, and it is so important. What does it mean? It simply means setting aside specific times to focus on how you will improve your business through phone calls, mailings, emails, and face-to-face communication with people who can help you bring in more business. Who are these people?

1. YOUR Sphere of Influence (SOI):

One of the best lead-generating tools is right in your own backyard. That is, your own personal sphere of influence, the people you know. Some sources for these people might come from:

- family
- friends
- neighbors
- place of worship
- school
- children's sport activities
- civic associations you belong to
- golf or tennis partners
- local Chamber of Commerce
- other organizations you belong to
- people you see every day at the grocery store, etc.

As a newer agent, you need to let your contacts know that you are in the real estate business. If you are a seasoned agent, then your contacts and past clients need to be reminded that you are still in the business. A newer agent can start with a letter of introduction or announcement that gets mailed to your contacts.

Always include something of value or interest to them. For example, provide the current statistics from your MLS on the homes sold in their neighborhoods. (Everyone loves to see their local statistics.) Don't forget to ask for their business, and include your business card.

2. Monthly newsletters/mailings to your sphere and neighborhood

There are many companies that publish newsletters which, for a fee, you can purchase, and I have used several of them. However, when you're just starting off in this business or trying to regroup, funds might be tight, so create your own.

When I first got into the business, I created a simple newsletter (one 8.5x11 page folded over, which produces a four-page product). It was titled "Dianne's Real Estate Corner," and it had my contact information on the front, local statistics for the neighborhood and MLS on the inside pages, and a food recipe on the back. I used this tactic again after my stint as a successful Realtor® in the northern Virginia area for 20 years; I found myself starting all over again when I moved to North Carolina where I didn't know many people. So, I went back to basics and started the simple newsletter again.

Everyone loves to view the latest real estate statistics about their local area. They want to know how many homes are on the market for sale, how many have sold, and what was the selling price. They want to know how long these properties took to sell. All you need to do is take the time to create a template (or if you're not very computer-savvy, then have one of your children or a friend create this for you). After the template is created, it can be used month after month by just changing the statistics and the date.

I find that including one of my favorite recipes on the last page of the newsletter helps to make the newsletter a little more personal. I'm certain that some people read it, because one woman in my neighborhood called me to ask what the oven temperature should be for the apple butter cake recipe — a bit of information that apparently I forgot to include!

3. Open houses

Open houses may seem like an old idea, but if you plan properly, they can prove to be rewarding for making new contacts. If you don't have a good listing, volunteer to hold an open house for another agent in your office, but be selective and make sure the property has a good location and a good price range; you also should preview the property in advance. Be sure to keep a list of the names and contact information of the potential clients who attend your open house and add them to your mailing list.

Sellers believe that open houses will sell their property, but the truth is that, many times, an open house helps the agent more than the sellers. The agent has the opportunity to meet neighbors and other people who stop by, and these can be the agent's potential buyers and sellers for future transactions.

I have held many open houses over the past 30 plus years, and only two buyers actually bought the house I was hosting. However, the benefit to me was that I was able to meet more prospects face-to-face, establish a relationship with them, and therefore work with them on future buyer and seller transactions.

> → *TIP: I've discovered that some people are reluctant to give you their phone number; however, they will more readily give you their email address. So, following their name, that's the first thing I ask for.*

The following Open House Guide will help you plan it:

OPEN HOUSE GUIDE
**Open House Reception is all about the opportunity to meet
Prospective Buyers and Sellers!**

- **Prepare ahead!**
  - ☐ Bring enough Brochure Copies, and Guest Register forms.
  - ☐ Directional Signs & Open House signs.
  - ☐ Check for Ad in paper
  - ☐ Bring your laptop (don't forget your power cord).
  - ☐ Bring copies of recent Sales in the neighborhood, OR display them on your laptop!
  - ☐ Bring copies of other homes For Sale in the neighborhood
  - ☐ Bring plenty of business cards or Personal promotional items to give away (your personal brochure, pens, key chains, etc.)
  - ☐ Vacant house? - Bring a card table and 2 folding chairs.
  - ☐ Hold a drawing for a plant? - A Gift Certificate? - Bring forms for drawing
  - ☐ Refreshments?
  - ☐ Ask your favorite Loan Officer to prepare sample financing plans for the property.
  - ☐ SAFETY FIRST! Make certain that a family member or the office knows where you are, and remember to take your cell phone with you (with full battery charge).

- **Arrive Early!**

- Welcome guests with openness, warmth and sincerity. Shake hands and SMILE!

- Guide Guests to the Display Table, and ask them to sign the Guest Registry "for the seller".

- As you tour the home, don't announce the obvious ("This is the kitchen . . . "), but do point out features that guests might miss.

- Examples of "consultative questions" to evaluate their real estate needs.
  - How did you find out about the Open House?
  - Where are you living now?
  - Are you working with another Realtor?
  - How long have you been looking for a home?
  - Of the homes you have seen, which ones did you like best (and why)?
  - Do you have a house to sell? (Is your house currently listed?)
  - What features do you like about your home? . . . What don't you like about your home?
  - How many people are in your household?
  - Have you been pre-approved for a mortgage? (Would you like me to arrange an appointment for you with a mortgage representative?)
  - How do you like this home?
  - What questions do you have?
  - I'm sure that I can find you several homes with the features you're interested in. Would you be available after I close my Open House, or would later in the week be better?

- **Follow Up after the Open House,** and send thank you notes to all the people who signed your guest registry.

- **DON'T FORGET**: Add all names and information to your database, and keep them on your mailing list!

GOOD LUCK, AND GOOD PROSPECTING!

Another way to locate buyers and sellers is called "farming", or I prefer to call it "marketing." It simply means that you take a specific geographic neighborhood, or a specific group of people, and send out (or hand deliver) information on a regular basis (preferably at least once a month). We will discuss this in more detail in Chapter 11.

Internet marketing is a big source in our current market, and I'll cover this in more detail in Chapter 16.

TAKE ACTION!

1. Write down a list of all the people you know (your Sphere of Influence).
2. Select a two-hour per day time frame in which you lead-generate by calling or mailing to your sphere.
3. Start preparing a simple newsletter to send out.
4. Prepare and schedule an Open House.

Farming, aka
Marketing for Business

In the real estate business, there are several different types of farming, which is another term for marketing. These terms mean consistently communicating to a group of potential clients. The group can be the people you know from specific organizations that you belong to, or it can be contacts from a geographical area. If you are considering a geographical area, then the best place to start might be your own neighborhood. Or, if you prefer to work with first-time buyers, then you might want to consider a nice apartment complex where you would meet people who are considering their first home.

When I first moved to North Carolina, I had no Sphere of Influence and no business. Ours was the tenth house built in the neighborhood of 825+ lots that made up our community. While it was a small but growing neighborhood at that time, I decided to prepare and deliver a monthly newsletter. Each home had a mailbox with a newspaper box attached below. Since it is illegal to put anything but mail in a U.S. mail box, we delivered the newsletters to the paper boxes each month.

As the number of homes increased, so did the newsletters, and so did my business. When our community was completed, about seven years later, I was doing about 35 percent of all the business in my neighborhood!

There are a few key elements that you should understand before you start marketing/farming:

1. Your branded information or newsletter should be delivered on a consistent basis — every month, if you're considering a monthly newsletter. I read a reputable survey that stated that if you send mailings fewer than eight times per year, you are probably wasting your time and money. Therefore, it is very important for you to be consistent and patient; don't give up after six months.

2. By "branding," I mean setting up your information or newsletter with the same style, photos, and logo, etc., every month, so that people will recognize you. You want to become known as the real estate expert in that neighborhood.

3. You need to extensively research the neighborhood of interest. Keep charts on the MLS statistics, and be able to quote the

average appreciation or depreciation or the number of sales during a specific timeframe. You need to know the floor plans of the different builders who built homes in that area. If applicable, you also need to become familiar with covenants of the specific neighborhood: what types of fences (if any) are allowed, are pets required to be on a leash, etc. You need to know about the schools in the neighborhood and where they are located. If it's a golf community, then you need to know about the club and fees for golfing, pools, etc. If you do your research and know everything that is pertinent to real estate in a particular neighborhood, then you will become known as the "Expert," and business will surely follow.

After my simple newsletter became a hit, I moved up to more professional types of e-newsletters and mailings.

♦ I subscribed to the Realty Times e-newsletter. The first two columns about current real estate topics are already prepared. The third column can be personalized, so I added a short introduction each month and included the current MLS statistics for that month. This newsletter was automatically emailed to all past clients, as well as to everyone in my database.

◆ I started snail-mailing a jumbo postcard (8.5 x 5.5), printed in color on both sides and laminated. One side showed my new listings and sales for the month, and the other side showed statistics, along with different promotions for that month. This postcard was sent to all past clients, current sellers, and my geographical marketing area.

The following are two samples of my jumbo postcard mailers to a neighborhood:

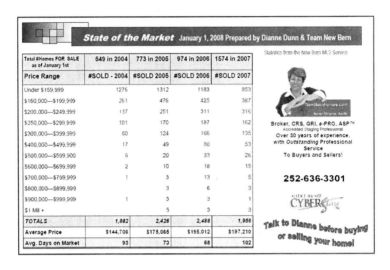

State of the Market January 1, 2008 Prepared by Dianne Dunn & Team New Bern				
Total #Homes FOR SALE as of January 1st	549 in 2004	773 in 2005	974 in 2006	1574 in 2007
Price Range	#SOLD - 2004	#SOLD 2005	#SOLD 2006	#SOLD 2007
Under $159,999	1276	1312	1183	853
$160,000—$199,999	261	476	425	387
$200,000—$249,999	137	251	311	316
$250,000—$299,999	101	170	187	162
$300,000—$399,999	80	124	166	135
$400,000—$499,999	17	49	80	53
$500,000—$599,900	6	20	33	26
$600,000—$699,999	2	10	18	15
$700,000—$799,999	1	3	13	5
$800,000—$899,999		3	6	3
$900,000—$999,999	1	3	3	1
$1 Mil +		5	3	3
TOTALS	1,882	2,426	2,488	1,956
Average Price	$144,706	$175,085	$195,012	$197,210
Avg. Days on Market	93	73	68	102

Statistics from the New Bern MLS Service

Broker, CRS, GRI, e-PRO, ASP™
Accredited Staging Professional
Over 30 years of experience,
with *Outstanding* Professional Service
To Buyers and Sellers!

252-636-3301

ALLEN TATE
CYBER*Homes*

Talk to Dianne before buying or selling your home!

What's
Home Staging?

View it all at
NewBernHomes.com
Tips for Sellers!

Just Listed!
026 Alexis Dr—Lake Clermont
$345,900

Pending!
117 Geneva Rd, Taberna
List price, $500,000

Just Listed!
1215 Pelican Dr—FFH
$365,900

Just Listed!
150 Perrytown Road—$150,000

Tours, Photos and more information at
www.NewBernHomes.com

YOUR COMPANY LOGO HERE 🏠

If your property is currently listed with another broker, please disregard this notice, as we fully cooperate with all companies.

> **TAKE ACTION!**
> 1. Decide which type of "Farming" you want to pursue, i.e. a geographical neighborhood, your sphere of influence, past clients, or all of them.
> 2. Select and prepare a postcard or flyer format which you want to send out (email or snail-mail). Make sure that you have your "branding" on the postcard of flyer.
> 3. Be consistent, and make sure that these are prepared to go out on a monthly basis.

– 12 –

Working with Buyers

The mailings and newsletters generally get your name out to your neighborhood and the people in your Sphere of Influence. Now, what do you do when someone calls you about purchasing a home? I've seen agents panic when this happens, only because they are not prepared.

Do your homework

One of the biggest mistakes agents make is to meet a prospective buyer at the property the buyer calls about with little or no pertinent information about the property or the prospect. In other words, the agent hasn't done their homework. Whether the prospective buyer comes from a sign call, an ad call, an open house, an Internet inquiry, or from a referral from someone you know, you should have a printed checklist or script of questions ready to ask before you set up the appointment.

Team New Bern

BUYER-PROSPECT – QUESTIONNAIRE

Date: _____   Lead Source: _____

CONTACT INFO

Name:	Spouse:	
Email	Spouse:	
Street Address	Children (names/ages)	
Home Phone	Cell Phone	
Work Phone	Fax	
Best way to get in touch	Best times	

1. How did you find us?   Website, MilitaryByOwner site, Realtor.com site? Ad, Sign, Personal referral?
2. **Are you currently working with another Realtor here? Yes No**

3. **Are you under a signed Buyer Agent Agreement with another Realtor?** _____

4. Have you visited the New Bern area before? **Yes No**   *If yes,* did you see any properties that you liked? _____. *If yes,* **your reason for not purchasing?**

5. **What is the time-frame that you would like to make a move here?** _____
6. Reason for your move? Job Transfer _____   Retiring _____   2ⁿᵈ Home _____
7. How many in your family? Adults _____   Children _____ Ages _____

8. What criteria are you looking for in a home? Size? _____ BR's? _____ Baths? _____ Single-Family or TH/Condo? _____ Is there anything else that is especially important to you? Golf? Boating? Sailing? Fishing?

9. What Price Range are you comfortable with $_____

10. **Do you need to sell a home first?** _____

11. **Method of financing: Will you be paying Cash or are you considering a Mortgage?** _____

    a. **Have you been pre-approved by a lender?** _____ Mortgage amount? $_____
    b. Down payment amount? $_____
    c. It is customary in this area to be pre-approved by a lender, which will give you the clout and leverage you need to secure the best price and terms for your new home.
    d. May we suggest a few reliable lenders and have them contact you? _____

12. When are you planning a visit to New Bern? _____

13. It's best that we set up an appointment, so that I can meet with you at my office, and review the search information that I'll be doing for you. **Which is the better time for us to meet, the day you arrive, or the next day?**

Appointment Date and Time: _____

Other Information:

_____

_____

_____

In addition, you should suggest that they get pre-approved for their loan, if they are financing the property. Being pre-approved is different from pre-qualified. Pre-qualified means that they have spoken with a lender, whereas pre-approved means that they made an application, their credit rating has been reviewed, and if all the information they provided is verified by the lender, then they can be approved for a specific loan amount.

While some potential buyers may balk at pre-approval, my typical answer is that having a lender's letter accompany any contract offer gives them leverage over other buyers who do not. In addition, they may possibly get a better price and terms if the seller knows up front that they are truly qualified to purchase the property.

When I receive calls on a property from potential buyers, I feel that an exchange of information is very important. Otherwise, we may both be wasting our time. The buyer prospect wants their questions answered, and I want information from the buyer before I can help them. I call that system "answering a question with a question," and I'm sure that many of you have heard that concept. It goes like this:

> *Prospect: "What price is the house on the corner of XYZ street?"*
>
> *Agent: "That's a great property on a ¾ acre lot, and is being offered for $250,000. Is that a price range that you're comfortable with?"*

OR

> *Prospect: "How many bedrooms and bathrooms does it have?"*

Agent: *"This lovely property has 2 bedrooms and 1.5 baths on the main level, and 1 bedroom plus a full bath on the upper level. It's approximately 2300 heated square feet. Is that the size home you're looking for?"*

In both scenarios, you can see that I am answering their questions honestly, and also asking them if this fits their needs. Most of the time, I have found that people will often relax a little and share with you that the price range may be too high for them. When that happens, you can follow up by asking them what their comfortable price range is.

You'll notice that I use the word "comfortable"; that's an automatically relaxing word. I'm not asking them how much they can afford, or how much money they make. I'm asking them what price range they feel comfortable with. Some people can afford to purchase a higher priced home but do not want to strap themselves with a big mortgage, so this type of scenario shows that you are truly trying to help them in their search while staying within their parameters.

The next important step is getting the appointment, and this should be conducted in your office. I call it the Buyer Consultation appointment, and have a pre-printed package ready to review and give them.

The buyer consultation

This generally takes about one hour. I first welcome them and try to develop a friendly rapport through anything we might have in common that will bring about a sense of trust. It's very important to find out if this is their first purchase in your state. I have learned through experience that some people have bought and sold several properties and think they know it all; however, the process in each state can be different, and it is your job to educate them on how it works in your marketplace.

Our state has an agency law, so one of the first discussions we have is about how the different forms of agency work in North Carolina. To keep it simple and in layman's terms, I have prepared a chart that explains all of the three types of agency concepts in our state, along with the types of representation they can choose. After that, most prospective buyers are more than willing to sign the state disclosures, and even the Buyer Agency Agreement, which states that my company and I are working exclusively for the buyer for a specified time period, unless we enter into a dual-agency position. Consequently, it is very important for you, as the agent, to fully understand the provisions that your state follows.

After the disclosures are reviewed, I explain how the home-buying process works in our area and show the prospective buyer a checklist of the things that will happen from the day we start previewing homes to the day they find the home of their choice and, finally, to the date of their closing or settlement on the property. This is also the time to prepare them for any delays that might happen, which might be out of your control. However, you can assure them that by hiring you as their agent, you will do your very best to follow up on the entire process, and keep them updated.

Because closing costs vary in different counties or states, I provide a sample closing-cost chart, showing three different price ranges and what their average costs would be. I leave the fourth column blank until they find the home of their choice, and then I'll fill in that column with an estimate. I always caution them that these are only estimates, and that they will receive a "Good Faith Estimate" from their lender when they make a full loan application.

Since customer service is a very important part of my business, I also provide prospective out-of-state buyers with a list of vendors (home inspectors, surveyors, appraisers, lenders, etc.) along with my personal list, ranging from physicians to hair dressers. I find that people are extremely grateful to have this information, since they have no clue where to start, and they don't know any neighbors yet.

I also show them the areas and neighborhoods we will be covering on a large map on the wall. I explain that these properties were chosen based on the initial information that they gave me by phone or email.

The following pages are samples of the materials that are included in my Buyer's Consultation Package, and are given to the buyer in a pocket folder.

After reviewing the packet, I share with the buyers that the home-buying process should be non-stressful and fun, and that I have a system that I hope they will enjoy!

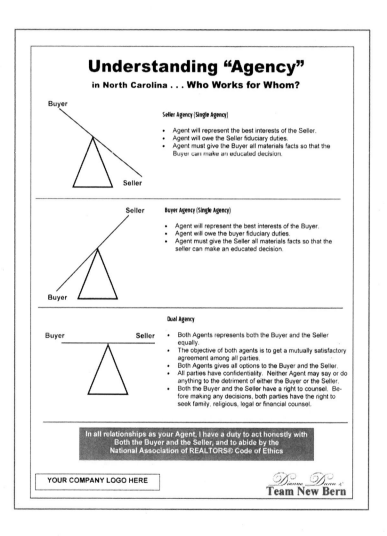

The Home Buying Process in North Carolina:

Dianne Dunn & Team New Bern

Presented by Dianne Dunn & Team New Bern,
Keller Williams® Realty 252-636-3301 or Toll Free 888-781-8800

Our Team has designed this chart to help you understand the home-buying process in North Carolina.

We understand the many questions and concerns of home buyers and how this information will be helpful throughout the transaction. We assure you that our #1 Priority is to provide you with the most professional and timely service available, so please feel free to contact us whenever you have a question — We're here to help!

Approximate Timeline From Day 1

Consultation to analyze YOUR needs
↓
Establish a working relationship (Buyer Agency Agreement)
↓
Financial Pre-Approval with Lender → Mortg. Application → Credit Report, OR → Decide to pay Cash
↓
View Properties that fit YOUR criteria
↓
Select Home → Market Analysis with your Agent
↓
Present Offer → Earnest Money Deposit (deposited within 24 hours of acceptance)

Contract

Acceptance of Contract → Inspections → Remove Contingencies
↓
Lender Appraisal → Loan Verifications
↓
Lender Underwriting → Rejection OR Conditions
↓
Loan Approval
↓
Closing Attorney → Title exam, Insurance, Survey
↓
Preparation of Documents/Attorney
↓

Approximately 30-60 Days

Closing (Recording of Deed) Possession following Recording → **Moving Day!**

Has the Housing Market Hit Bottom Yet?

- **In the graph below, the "V" represents the housing market.** The left side represents the market going **Down** to the "V-point", and the right side represents it going **Up**.

- **If we were to ask you where the housing market is right now, most would probably select somewhere near the Red Arrow marked 2010.**

- **How do we know when it actually hits the bottom?** Experience tells us that the housing market has hit the bottom when prices start to go back up. It will be difficult to find the exact bottom, since it's not a sudden shift. . . . *It's a gradual shift.*

- **You'll be able to tell when the market has turned when prices reach somewhere near the Green Arrow.**

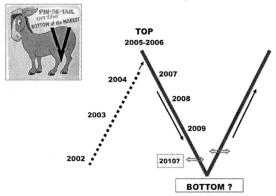

What's the difference in housing prices between the Red and Green Arrow? Not Much . . . *But there is another difference and it's major.*

If you buy a home on the left side of the graph, it is considered a *Buyers market.* You would be more likely to get concessions from sellers or builders including price reductions, repairs, upgrades, closing costs, etc.

If you wait until the market turns and you buy on the upswing, you and every other buyer who has been waiting for the market to hit bottom will be bidding on the same house. Those types of situations create a *Sellers market.*

There really is no better time to buy than now, for a few reasons:
1. There's a wonderful selection of homes to choose from right now.
2. Sellers are very willing to negotiate on price, terms and perks.
3. Interest rates are still at historic lows.

AVOID COMMON HOME-BUYING MISTAKES
Don't Let Your Home Purchase Go Wrong

Even with all the information available about buying homes, we in the Real Estate industry see consumers making some of the same mistakes, over and over again. As you are looking to make either your first or next home purchase, check out our list of mistakes you can avoid, to save money and hassles.

1. **Looking at Houses without first getting Loan Approval.** In today's marketplace, touring houses you think you would like to buy without knowing your buying power is a waste of everyone's time. It is discouraging for any buyer to fall in love with a house and write up a contract only to find out he or she can't afford the dream home. Getting loan pre-approval, however, is like having a credit card in your pocket for the purchase price. It gives you more clout with seller negotiations, eliminates surprises and saves valuable time.

2. **Buying the Wrong type of Home.** Many times, we've seen buyers purchase a home that has one characteristic they like, but none other. It might have a great kitchen, but overall it's too small (or too large). The price is great, but the house is too far from work. It's a perfect fixer-upper, but the buyers aren't handy with tools. Be sure to review every aspect of the house and compare it, not only with your "wants" list, but also your "lifestyle" list.

3. **Purchasing Without a Home Inspection.** In a steamed-up market, some buyers will consider forgoing a home-inspection contingency so their contract looks better than their competitors'. Although this may be necessary in a hot market, it can come back to bite the buyer (even the seller). Some sellers have wound up in court after accepting a contract without a home inspection. After-sale inspections of their homes revealed serious defects, prompting the buyers to take legal action for relief. If you're the buyer, you can go to court in such cases, but there's no guarantee you'll ever be compensated for the needed repairs or your court costs.

4. **Survey Surprises.** We're seeing more cash purchases of homes than ever before, which removes one of the common safeguards required by mortgage lenders (the property survey). Some Lenders require surveys to ensure there are no property-line problems. Many times a survey can show defects, such as a neighbor's fence placed over the line or violations of zoning regulations. If these are discovered, the seller should be responsible for correcting them, not the buyer.

5. **Buying Too Much Home.** Moving into a larger home usually seems like a good strategy for a growing family. But many people fail to realize that the new larger mortgage comes with new and larger home maintenance and repair costs. Energy costs are likely to be higher, along with yard upkeep expenses and cleaning costs. Think too, about how much it will cost you to furnish all the new space you have.

6. **Not looking at Different Loan Options.** Just as buyers look around at different houses on the market, they should also check out all the financing options available to them. Depending on your particular situation, the traditional 30-year, fixed interest rate loan may not be the best option for your home purchase. All loans are not created equal, and they sure don't cost the same. With banks and lending problems these days, make certain that you contact a lender who a good reputation for keeping their commitments and promises, and be very careful about selecting just any lender "online" who promises the lowest interest rate.

7. **Failing to use a Buyer's Agent.** It used to be that all real estate agents worked for sellers. In today's market, the buyer can hire an agent, too. This gives buyers someone in their corner, looking out after their best interests. Seller's and builder's agents, while required to treat buyers fairly and honestly, are compelled to negotiate in the best interests for their clients (the seller and the builder). Purchasing a home without a buyer's agent is like going to court without a lawyer.

8. **Not Reading the Fine Print.** Purchasing a home is the largest investment most of us ever make. That's why it's imperative to understand what you are signing! If you don't understand something about the sales contract, don't hesitate to ask for an explanation from your Buyer's Agent. The same advice applies to your mortgage loan.

We're here to answer any questions you may have, and to assist you in making the wisest choice for your next home purchase!

Dianne Dunn & Team New Bern
Keller Williams® Realty
Toll Free: 888-781-8800 Email: Info@NewBernHomes.com
Visit us on the Web at: www.NewBernHomes.com

Buyers - "Estimated" Closing Costs

The following examples of Buyers estimated closing costs have been prepared to assist you in computing your costs at closing of your new home. The examples are based on financing of a loan amount using a 20% downpayment of the Sales Price, with a 6% interest rate on the loan. NONE OF THESE FEES ARE CHARGED BY KELLER WILLIAMS REALTY, NOR IS KELLER WILLIAMS OR ITS AGENTS RECEIVING ANY PART OF THESE FEES. These fees are ESTIMATES ONLY; Actual charges should be confirmed with your Lender, Bank or Attorney.

Sales Price of House in each Price Range / Loan Amount:	$100,000 / $80,000	$200,000 / $160,000	$300,000 / $240,000	YOUR house Price
Loan Fees Charged by your Lender or Bank:				
Appraisal Fee (avg. $425, Paid when application is taken)	425	425	425	$
Credit Report (avg. $50, Paid when application ")	50	50	50	$
Loan Origination Fee (avg. 1% of loan amount, if applicable)	-	-	-	$
Underwriter/Document Review Fee (avg. $250-$400)	400	400	400	$
Processing fee (average $300-$600)	500	500	500	$
Flood Determination Fee (avg. $17-$25)	25	25	25	$
TAX Service Fee (avg. $85)	85	85	85	$
Courier Fee (average $30)	30	30	30	$
Items Required by Lender to be Paid in Advance:				
Interest on loan from day of closing to 1st day of next month (Est. 5 days @ $____/day)	78	156	233	$
Mortgage Insurance Premium (charged on loans with less than 20% downpayment, or some government loans)	-	-	-	$
Hazard Insurance Premium (Homeowners Policy, 1 year's premium usually paid prior to closing to the Insurance Company of your choice)	400	590	485	$
Flood Insurance Premium (if required)				$
POA (Property Owner's Association fee, if any - Prorated)				$
Reserves/Escrows deposited with Lender or Bank:				
Hazard Insurance: (3 months @ $____/month)	100	150	225	$
Mortgage Insurance: (___/months @ $____/month)	-	-	-	$
City/Town TAXES: (avg. 3-6/mos.) (___/months @ $____/month)	96	212	295	$
County TAXES (avg. 3-6/mos.) (___/months @ $____/month)	115	250	360	$
Title or Attorney Charges:				
Attorney Fee, including Title Examination (avg. $700-$750)	750	750	750	$
Title Insurance - (Lenders & Owner's coverage) ($2/$1,000 of sales price for 1st $100,000) ($1.50/$1,000 of sales price for next $400,000)	200	350	500	$
Notary Fee/Administrative charge (avg. $30-$50)	50	50	50	$
Express Mail fee for documents returned to your lender (avg. $40-$50)	50	50	50	$
Recording Fees:				
Deed: ($25)	25	25	25	$
Mortgage/Trust: ($85)	85	85	85	$
Additional Charges:				
Home Inspection Fee - (paid prior to closing - avg. $300-$450)	450	450	450	$
Survey (if required by Lender or requested - avg. $300-$400)	350	350	350	$
Termite/Pest inspection (required by Lender - avg. $100)	100	100	100	$
One Year Home Warranty (Optional - avg. $400-$500)	-	-	-	$
TOTAL Estimated Closing Fees:	**$4,364**	**$5,083**	**$5,473**	**$**

I have reviewed the Estimated Charges above, and acknowledge receipt of a copy of this form.

Buyer:_____ (date)_____ Buyer:_____ (date)_____

Prepared by _____ (date) _____

Team New Bern

Moving Tips
for a stress-free move!
☺

When you know the date you will be moving, remember to do the following:

☐1. If you are leasing your current home, **give written notice** to the landlord of your intent to move.

☐2. Contact all utility companies (telephone, gas, electric, water/sewer, cable, etc.) and schedule to disconnect at your current address, and reconnect at your new home as of the day of closing/settlement.

☐3. **Contact a moving company** (or several) and get cost estimates. Schedule your day to be packed and moved. If you are packing yourself, make sure to have plenty of boxes and packing paper on hand.

☐4. **Move on a weekday**, if you can, when banks, utilities and government offices are open.

☐5. **Contact your insurance company** for your new Homeowner's Insurance policy. They may ask several questions about the structure, etc., to estimate replacement value. Your REALTOR can assist you with some of these questions. Provide the policy to your lender, if you are financing your new home.

☐6. If you have school age children, **contact the current schools** and register the new schools.

☐7. If you are **moving out of state**, contact all medical doctors, dentists and other specialists that you or your family use, and ask for a referral physician in your new area.

☐8. **Transport with you** personally, any charts, x-rays, jewelry, passports, bank statements, checkbooks, or other important documents and items that you will need at your new location, whether they are for your home loan, children's schools, or any physicians. Arrange for extra refills on any prescriptions.

☐9. **Color code your boxes** by room, with self-stick colored labels and mark their contents. (e.g. green labels for all kitchen boxes, yellow for Master Bedroom, etc.) On the day of your move, give the movers a copy or quick sketch of your floor plan with the color code for each room (make sure to include codes for attic, garage, and storage room).

☐10. **Prepare an inventory** of your personal property (a home video would be best to accompany this list). (This could be invaluable in case of a fire or theft).

☐11. **Do Not pack** your bank statements or pay stubs for the last 6 months. Your new lender may need this information if you are financing your new home. They will provide you (at application) with a list of documents that will be needed by them, either before or at closing.

☐12. **Fill out change of address form** with the Post Office, and notify in writing, your address change for bank accounts, retirement accounts, securities accounts, magazine subscriptions, licenses, etc.

☐13. **Order preprinted address labels** with your new address as soon as you know it. (This will make the change of address process much easier!)

☐14. **Never make a move without wardrobe boxes!** Not only can you move clothes directly from closet to closet, but there's room on the bottom of the box for shoes, throw pillows and linens.

☐15. **Keep a utility log** to check service transfer dates. If you are moving locally, leave the power on at your old address so that you can go back and clean up after your move. OR, arrange for a cleaning crew to handle this for you.

☐16. **Important Final Tip:** Always pack a box or suitcase for each member of the family which contains one or two of the following: toothbrush, toothpaste, change of clothing, plastic cups, paper plates, napkins, utensils, coffee pot, filters and coffee, some beverages, toilet paper, paper towels, tissues, medications, extra light bulbs, and a towel and washcloth. If you have a pet, don't forget their dish and extra food! *No matter how organized you are, a move is always tiring. As soon as your movers leave, you will not feel like searching endlessly through boxes, for the basic necessities!*

It's important that you have the prospective buyers ride with you rather than take separate cars. This gives you a chance to build on your rapport and offers time for questions and answers about the area.

The next item I give clients is a clip board with MLS copies of each property that we will see. They are numbered on the top to correspond to the map that I give them, showing them where the properties are located. Stapled to the top of each MLS sheet is a "Property Rating Sheet." I have found that after most people see three properties, the features don't stand out any longer; they can't recall which place is which, and it sometimes becomes confusing. The Property Rating Sheet allows them to make their own individual notes as we preview each home. The ratings are set as 1, 2, or 3. After we preview the fourth home, I ask them to select their first three choices and to discard the fourth. We continue to do this as we see all the properties. I take their discarded sheets and throw them on the floor of my car, so we're not tempted to review them again!

Several years ago, I discovered that if I'm working with a couple, they each may have different opinions (as we all know!). So, I changed the form to include "Her Rating" and "His Rating" so they can both put down their own ratings. In the end, it is up to them to come to a common agreement.

PROPERTY RATING SHEET - Address:_____
(Compliments of Dianne Dunn & Team New Bern, Keller Williams® Realty)

To assist you in making a wise choice in your home selection, and to help you remember details on each property,
I have included this Property Rating Sheet. Please feel free to make any notes that will be helpful to you.

(Useful Tip: After you preview the first three properties, rate them according to your 1st, 2nd and 3rd choices. Then, as you see additional
properties, discard any, except for your top three choices).

This Property Rated:	
Her Rating:	#._____
His Rating:	#._____

1. Location _____
2. Interior Condition: _____
3. Bedrooms and
   Baths:_____
4. Kitchen:_____
5. Garage and/or Workshop:_____
6. Exterior and Yard:_____

Other Comments:_____

The rating sheet has turned out to be fun for most people, and they seem to like the system. It helps them eliminate properties while the features are fresh in their minds, and it helps me to eliminate the ones they didn't care for. In addition, I have found that having a back-up is very important, especially in a seller's market, just in case their first choice already has an offer in process. This system has saved all of us time and frustration.

When the buyers have narrowed down their choices, I ask them if they're prepared to make an offer on their first choice. If they need more time to think about it, then I don't pressure them. Rather, I encourage them to go back to their hotel room and make a list of all the pros and cons of the homes they are considering, and I set up a time to meet with them again in the morning.

Contract to Closing

This is probably the most critical part of a Realtor's® responsibility, since any glitches in the process are generally blamed on us. If you don't have an assistant to help you with this process, then you need your own checklist of items to be completed before the property can go to closing or settlement. During this time frame (generally 30 to 60 days from contract), it is extremely important to keep the buyer updated on the numerous tasks that are involved (inspections, appraisals, surveys, re-inspections, title work, etc.), so they know that you are working on a smooth closing for them.

For buyers and sellers, I email or mail a written checklist called "What Happens Next" so that they can follow along with the numerous tasks involved for the agents. It also has a checklist for what they need to gather and do before closing — things like getting their insurance in place, calling the utility company, the phone company, etc.

To keep track of the tasks, you can use a paper checklist or a management database, as I have for years (Top Producer, Agent Office, etc.). These systems are computerized and easy to use once you have your systems set up.

Thank you for allowing me and Team New Bern to assist
you with the purchase of your new property!

What Happens Next?
Here's my Check List/Action Plan to assist you towards a smoother Closing

Please note that some of the following items may not apply to land or lots.

PAPERWORK:

☑ You will receive a copy of the final Offer to Purchase and Contract, signed and initialed by all parties.

☑ Your earnest money deposit will be placed into the escrow account of the Listing Company, to be held until closing OR, a mutual release agreement is signed by both parties.

HOME INSPECTION:

☑ If specified in the Contract, your home inspection will be ordered by us, and the fee for the inspection needs to be paid directly to the inspector, prior to the home inspection.

☑ You will be notified of the date and time of the inspection. Home inspections generally take about 1½ to three hours, depending upon the size of the home. You do not need to be present during the inspection, but may choose to do so.

☑ Within a few days after the home inspection, you and I will receive a copy of the written report from the inspector by email, detailing the condition of the house, and listing any deficiencies noted. (Please don't be surprised by a long, detailed list of deficiencies, as many home inspectors feel compelled to list every item, regardless of how minor they are).

☑ You will review the report, and it's part of our job to assist you in making decisions on repair items that you want the Seller to correct. The home's major components that the Seller is responsible for are covered in Paragraphs 13(a) and 13(c) of the contract. Any other items are considered "negotiable" between you and the Seller, and the Seller is not obligated to correct these.

☑ If there are any deficiencies that you want the Seller to correct, they will be listed on the standard NCAR Repair Agreement, signed and dated by you, and I will have a copy delivered to the Seller's Realtor within the time specified in the contract.

☑ The Seller will then have a specified number of days to respond to the Repair Agreement.

TERMITE/PEST INSPECTION:

☑ If specified in the Contract, a termite/pest inspection will be ordered for you. This inspection generally costs $100-$125 and is charged to you on the closing statement, and you will be given a copy at the time of closing. You do not need to be present for the Termite/Pest Inspection.

☑ If any evidence of pest infestation or damage is listed on the inspector's report, then the Seller will be responsible for treatment and/or any damage repair by a licensed pest control company, in accordance with Paragraph 12(c) of the contract. We suggest that you maintain an annual Warranty contract with a licensed pest control company, so that your property will be inspected annually.

APPRAISAL:

☑ The appraisal is ordered by your Lender. After the appraiser's report is complete, it will be sent to the Closing Attorney and you will be given a copy at closing. We will be notified ONLY if there is a problem with the appraisal meeting the contract price.

ATTORNEY PREPARATION FOR CLOSING:

☑ We will send a copy of your contract and any other pertinent information to the Closing Attorney's office and request a time for closing. They will order a title search on the property, to ensure that you receive a clear deed. They will also prepare the necessary documents from instructions that are sent to them by your lender.

-2-

☑ The attorney will also prorate all annual property taxes between the Buyer and Seller. (City and County taxes are paid in arrears, so that taxes will be due from the Seller from January 1 until the day of closing. The attorney collects taxes for the remainder of the year from the Buyer, and disburses to the appropriate government tax office). If there is any POA (Property Owner's Association) fee, that will also be prorated at closing.

☑ You will be notified of the date, time, and contact numbers for the attorney. The actual closing generally takes one hour or less. If necessary, you can make arrangements with the attorney's office to sign all of your closing documents by mail, if you cannot attend the closing. Please make certain that your lender is aware that you will not be attending.

OUR FOLLOW-UP PROCESS UNTIL CLOSING:

☑ We have a follow-up system in place, where we will check with the Seller's Realtor and the Closing Attorney, to make certain that all of the above reports, documents and information are received in a timely manner.

BUYER'S FINAL WALK-THRU:

☑ According to paragraph 14 of the contract, the Buyer has the right to schedule a final "Walk-Thru" of the property just before closing. This will be scheduled at a time that's convenient for all parties.

☑ We will request that the Seller leave any garage door openers, instruction manuals for appliances, irrigation systems, security systems, etc. in the house for you.

BUYER'S CHECKLIST FOR CLOSING:

☐ **Payment check for Home Inspection?** (Generally $375-$500—depending upon size of home) - check is due at home inspection, made payable to inspection company)

☐ **Loan Application taken?** (Contact your lender within 3 days of contract acceptance)

☐ **Attorney Selected?** (Immediately after contract acceptance—we will assist you with names)

☐ **Power of Attorney needed for closing?** (Arrange with lender & attorney's office as soon as possible)

☐ **Termite inspection company selected?** (Immediately after contract acceptance—Team NB can make arrangements)

☐ **Do you want a new survey plat of the lot?** (Immediately after contract acceptance—Team NB can make arrangements)

☐ **Obtain Homeowner's Insurance Policy?** (Contact your insurance company at least 3 weeks before closing).

☐ **Obtain Flood Insurance Policy, if required?** (At least 3 weeks before closing)

☐ **Call utility companies to set up accounts and change over to your name?** (2 weeks before closing)

☐ **Call phone company for service?** (2 weeks before closing)

☐ **Call TV cable company (optional)?** (2 weeks before closing)

☐ **Arrange for certified funds for closing?** (Call attorney's office 2 days before closing)

Utility Companies and Services:		Need Help with Insurance Companies? The following are Insurance Agents that we recommend:
City of New Bern	(252) 636-4070 (Water, Electric,Trash & Recycling)	
CP&L	(800) 452-2777 (Natural Gas & elec. in some areas)	1.
Sprint	(252) 633-9011 (Telephone service)	2.
Cox Communications	(252) 638-3121 (Cable TV, or high-speed Internet Service)	3.
Propane Gas	(252) 637-3903 (Amerigas) (252) 633-5560 (Jenkins Gas & Oil)	

Please print this checklist and keep this information handy as a reference.
Feel free to contact our Closing Coordinator if you have any questions!
Congratulations on the Purchase of your New Home!

Dianne Dunn & Team New Bern

One of the biggest complaints from buyers and sellers after a contract has been signed is that they don't hear from their agent. Most of the time, that's because the agent has moved on to the next buyer, and the closing paperwork and tasks slide through the cracks. You must keep the channels of communication open and keep your clients updated on the complete process if you want a smooth closing — and repeat or referral business.

TAKE ACTION!

1. Prepare a Buyer Consultation Package
2. Practice your scripts with prospective buyers.
3. Prepare a checklist for closing

Working with Sellers

Listings have always been my favorite. Some agents feel that all you need to do for a listing is follow "The Three P's": Put up the sign, Put it in MLS, and Pray! A truly professional Listing Agent, however, is responsible for state-of-the-art marketing to get the property sold.

When I first receive a call from a prospective seller, I also use a checklist questionnaire to find out more information about the property, why they are moving, their time frame for moving, etc. These are all very important questions that will help you with your marketing.

Pre-Listing package

As soon as an appointment is established, I email (or hand deliver to them) my Pre-Listing Package. (If I email it, I also bring a printed version with me to the appointment.) I like to give them a chance to see how my team and I work and what to expect. My title of the package is "Services Proposal"; it contains about 21 colorful pages, spiral bound with a plastic cover in front and back. It consists of:

- A cover page with team photo and my personal contact information.
- "Meet Dianne" — This is my bio page along with my professional designations, my memberships on boards and committees, and the number of properties I've sold over the past year. It's like a "brag" page that sellers can read in advance, so you don't need to brag when you meet them.
- "Meet Dianne's Team" — If you have a team, then add a page with photos of each team member, their titles, and the services they provide for your sellers.
- "How to Select a Realtor®" — On this page I encourage the sellers to ask questions of all Realtors® they are interviewing, and I provide some sample questions, along with my answers, for example:

  ◇ How many years experience do you have?
  ◇ What is your average sales price?
  ◇ What is your average days on the market (compared to your MLS)?
  ◇ Do you have a personal website? (not a company site)

◊ What are the statistics of website traffic that you receive?

◊ Do you have a Written Marketing Plan, and how will you market my home?

When I was a newer agent and didn't have a track record behind me, I used the statistics of my company. (Hopefully, you are associated with a successful company.) To counter the seasoned agent's approach, I shared with the seller that, while I did not have a track record "yet," I had the dedication, enthusiasm, energy and time to devote to their listing, and asked them to give me the chance to prove it.

♦ "Web Statistics" — This page shows statistics from my site and demonstrates how important search engine placement is on the Internet in order for you to be easily found. I encourage the seller to "Google" for themselves and view the results. I make certain that my site always comes up on page 1, and is generally in the top five.

♦ "Why List with Me?" — Here I list ten good reasons, including all the different marketing that I do to expose their property to a number of prospective buyers.

♦ Advertising on REALTOR.com — I show them copies of how a listing looks with only one photo, and then show them the Showcase

Listings that are enhanced with 25 photos and that also cost the listing agent an additional fee. I want the sellers to know that I'm willing to spend money on marketing to give them the best exposure.

◆ "Just Listed" announcements — Clients see a copy of an email blast that goes out to over 2,000 people in my database. It contains photos, virtual tours, etc.

◆ Feedback responses — This is a page on the electronic system that I use for gathering feedback from agents who have shown a property. (In the early years of these systems, many agents in my area did not use email frequently, so I used to offer an incentive. If you replied to the email questionnaire within two days, then your name was entered into a quarterly $50 drawing. The response rate went up dramatically.)

◆ "The Importance of Intelligent Pricing"—The next few pages cover pricing and how important it is to price their property right the first time, especially in a buyer's market, or they won't be in the range of being shown.

◆ "What will this COST me?" — This page explains real estate fees/commissions and how they work. I use a sample dollar bill to show where each percentage goes (seller's agent/company, buyer's agent/company). In addition, I itemize my personal expenses to show that I am truly running a business

— and that, contrary to what many sellers believe, I do not have the choice of keeping the entire commission for myself. Most of the time, this is an eye-opener for many sellers, who actually think that our companies pay for everything or that agents might be paid a salary, like other employees.

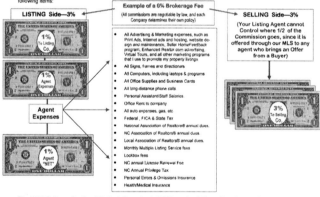

What will this COST me?

Allow me to Share with you: 1) How Realtors are Paid.   2) Where Commissions go.

The *"No Risk—No Reward"* factor contributes to the Fee Structure of the Real Estate Industry

REALTORS® are Independent Contractors, and Do Not receive a Salary—Realtors work strictly on a commission-basis, and are *only paid* when a property transaction has closed and the title has transferred. (*Salaried employees don't take Risks* — They are paid, regardless of what they do.)

A Realtor's® income is based *totally on Risk*: The typical buyer or seller does not invest any upfront money for a Realtor's® services. A Realtor invests Time—Marketing dollars—Expenses— Energy and Knowledge, without the guarantee of compensation, benefits, paid vacation, or employer-shared tax contributions.

Division of Brokerage Fees—When a Realtor earns a commission or brokerage fee:
- It is first divided between the real estate companies in the transaction (generally 50% to Listing Co. and 50% to Selling Co.)
- Next, the fee is divided between our local franchise (Keller Williams Realty), and the Listing agent.
- From that net fee, a 6% franchise fee is deducted and paid by the agent to Keller Williams International.
- The personal "Gross Income" check is paid to the agent, and the agent pays all of their own business expenses, including the following items:

LISTING Side—3%

Example of a 6% Brokerage Fee
(All commissions are negotiable by law, and each Company determines their own policy)

SELLING Side—3%
(Your Listing Agent cannot Control where 1/2 of the Commission goes, since it is offered through our MLS to any agent who brings an Offer from a Buyer)

- All Advertising & Marketing expenses, such as Print Ads, Internet ads and hosting, website design and maintenance, Seller HomeFeedback program, Enhanced Realtor.com advertising, Virtual Tours, and all other marketing programs that I use to promote my property listings
- All Signs, frames and directionals
- All Computers, including laptops & programs
- All Office Supplies and Business Cards
- All long-distance phone calls
- Personal Assistant/Staff Salaries.
- Office Rent to company
- All auto expenses, gas, etc
- Federal , FICA & State Tax
- National Association of Realtors® annual dues.
- NC Association of Realtors® annual dues.
- Local Association of Realtors® annual dues.
- Monthly Multiple Listing Service fees
- Lockbox fees
- NC annual License Renewal Fee
- NC Annual Privilege Tax
- Personal Errors & Omissions Insurance
- Health/Medical Insurance

Agent Expenses

- The *VALUE* of a professional Realtor's® service is *NOT* based on information alone — the consumer can search the Internet for most information.
- The *TRUE VALUE* of a professional Realtor's® service is:
  - The expert "interpretation" of the information.
  - Counseling of the client, based on that information.
  - The Skill of Negotiations, on behalf of their clients best interests.
- Can Real Estate Commissions be Reduced?
  Certainly! . . . However, if the fees in the real estate industry were to be reduced, then the consumer would need to assume *More of the RISK*, just like any other service that we elect to purchase:
  - *Buyers would be paying an hourly rate,* including the cost of expenses for investment of time, whether they purchase a home or not.
  - *Sellers would be paying up-front fees for marketing costs and time,* even if the home does not sell.

There will ALWAYS be Discounts in ANY industry, . . . And Only YOU can decide on the Quality of Service you expect to receive.

Dianne & Team New Bern—*We Offer Unparalleled SERVICE & RESULTS!*

17.

I feel strongly that we need to prove our worth to sellers. We need to show them the value of our services and how they might differ from our competition. In a competitive buyer's market, in which there's a high inventory of homes to choose from, in many cases, I've been able to secure a higher fee or commission by proving my value and worth and showing how we can offer a higher incentive to other buyer agents to show the property.

When sellers have asked if my commission is negotiable, I've answered in a few ways, always with a big smile:

"Absolutely! How much MORE would you like to pay me for my services?" Or ...

"Actually, my services are worth 20 percent, but I'll be happy to accept 10 percent!"

Most of the time, the sellers chuckle along with me and realize that, for the services I provide, I'm not willing to take less, especially in a buyer's market, where I can be expected to carry the listing expenses for several months or longer.

In some special cases, I have accepted a graduated commission compensation, where my fee was 5 percent for the first 30 days, and 5.5 percent for the next 30 days. If the property did not sell within 60 days, then we were back to my full compensation of 6 percent. I explain to the sellers that the longer their property is on the market, the higher my marketing expenses are. If I use the graduated compensation plan, then this is all written into the listing agreement that the sellers and I sign.

In one transaction that was a graduated commission, a seller received an offer on the 59th day. When they were ready to counter the offer, they realized that they would be paying ½ percent more anyway, so they elected to accept the offer as is.

Sometimes, when the property is in a neighborhood or price range with heavy competition, I will recommend adding a 1 percent bonus to the buyer side of the compensation as an incentive to increase the showings.

◆ "Staging" your home for sale — I call it "Showtime or Stage-it-to-Sell," and it lists all the tasks that they need to complete from interior to exterior. Also included are tips on showings, and several pages of "before and after" photos to demonstrate why staging is so important.

I mentioned the two-day course offered by Barb Schwarz of StagedHomes.com™, where I received valuable information on how to present this information to sellers, and how to actually stage a home.

While many sellers will tell me how much time and money they have spent on "decorating" and improvements, I like to share with them that decorating is actually "personalizing" the home for their own comfort and pleasure, and that staging is "de-personalizing" it so that the property will be more neutral and appealing to the majority of prospective buyers.

After this presentation, most of my sellers are willing to remove all the clutter (or the "refrigerator art," as I like to call it), clean off countertops, and complete a checklist of items that need to be done, prior to putting their house on the market. I remind them that they will be packing and moving anyway, so this is a good time to start packing up some items.

What is Staging?

There's a big difference between _STAGING_ a home and _DECORATING_ a home:

- Decorating is "Personalizing" a home for YOU to live in.

- Staging is the art of de-Personalizing a home, so that _ALL_ potential buyers can envision living there.

- Staging is a statistically proven method that typically sells homes faster and for more money.

- An accredited ASP™ can help!

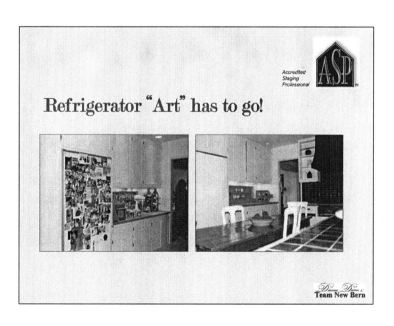

Bathroom Clutter must Be Eliminated, so the bathroom looks much Bigger!

Team New Bern

De-Cluttering Works Every Time!

Team New Bern

Some agents have told me, "Your listings always show so nicely. I wish my sellers would do that." My feeling is that it's the agent's responsibility to educate the seller on how to stage the house properly, and we can't do this unless we have the tools and examples to show them, along with confidence in our systems. Confidence in this business is crucial. The more we practice, the more we do it, and the better we get.

◆ "Closing Cost Statement" — I give the sellers a sample of the typical closing costs in our area, and I break my chart down to three different price ranges, based on the recent comparable homes sold. One is the listing price, the second is a middle range, and the last is the lowest price, also based on the most recent comparable sales. I leave the sellers a copy of these closing costs, and I keep one in my file that I can refer to when we receive an offer.

◆ "Sellers Homework" page — I use this to request a copy of items we will need from them for both marketing and closing: a recent survey, floor plan if available, title insurance, recent appraisal, name and contact of any lenders with outstanding liens, and a key that works easily to the front door.

I have actually had sellers state that they always enter their house through the side door or garage — that they never use the front door and have lost their key. Explain to the seller that for all showings, it is extremely important that the agent and prospective buyers be able to enter through the front door. The foyer and front area should be the most welcoming part of the house, and it gives the buyer a better feel for the "flow" of the house and the floor plan. I kindly ask them to either find the front door key or hire a locksmith to make a new one.

◆ I also include a page where they can list the last 12 months of utilities. Generally, the second question buyers ask after the price is what does it cost to heat and cool this house. Why wait for someone to ask — let's have it ready now.

◆ My final page in the package is a photo of my team, thanking the sellers for taking the time to review my proposal, and finishing with a quote "Experience and Service are NOT Expensive...They're Priceless!"

I've been using a Pre-Listing Package for many years — well before it became a popular item. Most sellers are very impressed with the time and effort that I have taken to prepare this, as well as with my track record.

Many times the sellers are interviewing two or three agents, and I agree that they should have choices before they hire an agent. While some agents like to be the first to present, I generally like to be the last, if possible. This sometimes gives me a chance to hear what other agents have advised them, and by being last, I have a better opportunity to leave with a signed listing agreement.

Along with the required paperwork and state disclosures for listing a property, I also bring to the appointment a preliminary Comparative Market Analysis (CMA), which I have researched and prepared, so that I can give them a general idea of the price range. I always give a price range for the house rather than a specific price. Sometimes it requires a second visit to get down to the specifics of pricing, after I have previewed the property and compared it to others that have recently sold.

There is one last point I'd like to share about working with sellers, and that's about using email for communication. I find it to be extremely efficient, and it allows me to keep a written record of communication and exchanges.

I've had agents tell me "Oh, maybe you work with high-tech sellers, but my sellers won't use email." My response is that, again, it's up to us to educate the sellers on the most efficient way to help them. Most of the younger people are already onboard with email, so that's not an issue. I work with many retirees and have discovered that these people usually have email, if only to communicate with their children and grandchildren. I always ask the seller for their email address (or addresses of both of them). If they say that they have one but don't use it much, then my "smiling response" is: "I understand, Mr. and Mrs. Seller; however, since most of our communication systems are designed for using email, it's really very important that you open your email at least once every day until we get your house sold. Is that agreeable to you?" I have had only one person who did not have email, but when I told them about the free email accounts available through hotmail or g-mail, they reconsidered.

Listing to contract

Here's where you can shine or become one of the statistics who lose the listing if the contract falls apart. Sellers want to hear from you. You need to understand that most sellers don't care if you are servicing 10 listings or 100 listings. They only care about one property: their own. Here are ways you can help them feel like they are your best clients:

- Keep in touch with them with weekly or bi-weekly phone calls, even if it is only to say that nothing has happened in their neighborhood. It proves to them that you are working for them and that their property is still a high priority for you.
- Send out or email reports on the how many people have viewed them on the website.

Those charts are an impressive way for the sellers to see how many people have previewed their property online.

♦ Send them copies of feedback reports from agents who have previewed or shown the property. While my sellers receive immediate email feedback with the program I use, I like to send a bi-weekly recap of the showings and the feedback replies. Sometimes there are issues that the seller or I have missed, and they can easily be corrected. Additionally, if the seller reads enough comments suggesting, for example, that the price is too high, then this can be another means of confirming your suggestion to lower the price.

♦ Send a monthly report on their neighborhood statistics, along with the MLS statistics. I have even used a comparison chart from the prior year to show the market trends. It only takes one template to prepare, and you can use it over again for each neighborhood that you list in.

♦ Add the sellers to your monthly email newsletter.

♦ Answer their calls promptly.

♦ When an offer comes in, be prepared with recent comparable sales in the neighborhood and a new net sheet showing their estimated closing costs.

➜ TIP: Do not enter your listing in MLS until you have all photos ready to upload, along with the proper disclosures, survey, floor plan, if applicable, and brochure, if you choose. I'm not suggesting that you violate your MLS rules about entry deadlines; I'm simply suggesting that you prepare this information in advance and have it ready. Like many other agents, when I open the MLS morning update, if I can't see all photos and information about the property, I skip it and go on to the next one. The chances of me coming back another day are slim, unless this property falls into a search that I'm specifically looking for.

Why do this? It's simple: It's a great time-management system for you. If all the photos and documents are uploaded to your MLS, then agents who are showing the property and need information can go directly to MLS and download it without calling or emailing you or your assistant. This is especially valuable on weekends, when you'd like some time off with your family.

It always amazes me when I see new property listings on the daily update, and there's either no photo or only one photo and no other information. The agent says "Oh, I'll add that later." Remember, some of us are just like a house-showing: you only get one chance to make a good first impression. Don't count on the agents remembering to go back to your listing next week to see what they should have seen on Day 1!

Be creative with your marketing

Whether you are using print ads or online ads for your listings, remember that you are selling a way of life, not just a place to live. Your advertising should be an attention-getter, a headline that attracts specific prospects. The ad needs to draw interest and offer a benefit to the reader so that they have a desire to contact you. You also need to draw action — make it easy for the reader to respond.

Rather than the regular description of "Beautiful home, 3BR, 2Bath, etc.," try some eye-catching sample headlines instead:

- Need More Elbow Room?
- All the Work's Done!
- Fresh as Spring!
- T-Bone Value — Hamburger Price!
- Opportunity Is Knocking!!
- Owner Packing — Quick Possession!
- Exceptionally Smart!
- Halfway to Heaven!
- Too Good to Last!
- Stunning Departure from the Ordinary!
- Practice Your Putting!
- Come Where It's Cool!
- Are You a Nature Lover?

Multiple offers

While the last few years have been a "Buyer's Market" in most parts of the country, there are occasions when multiple offers come in at the same time on a property that is extremely well-priced, or considered a great buy at the time.

When this happens, make sure that you review the NAR® Code of Ethics, Articles 1 and 3 so that you will be familiar with your obligations on how to be fair and ethical to all parties.

Some tips that I've used:

♦ When an offer comes in, review the entire document, check for all initials, signatures, dates and the earnest money deposit check.

♦ Contact your seller as soon as possible and set up an appointment to present the offer/offers. When you have multiple offers, I have found it best to arrange the appointment at the office, so that I had access to the MLS and copying facilities if needed.

♦ "Set the Stage" with the seller. Ask the seller if this is the first time they have sold a property in your state. If so, explain to them that you will be presenting ALL terms of each offer, and then you will both discuss each part of the offers.

♦ The final decision is always the sellers; however, with multiple offers, they might need your guidance on what terms are the most important to look for, etc.

Multiple offers can be emotionally taxing on both the seller and their agent, so to keep it simple and more organized, I prepared a Multiple Offer Comparison Chart to assist the seller in making their decision. In addition to the price, it shows the deposit, down payment, whether the buyer has lender approval, any contingencies affiliated with each offer, and the brokerage fee that each company is receiving. The bottom line shows the seller an estimated "net" before other types of loan payoff or closing costs.

MULTIPLE OFFER COMPARISON CHART

Property Address: _____ Seller: _____

OFFER #1	OFFER #2	OFFER #3
Buyer:	Buyer:	Buyer:
Realtor:	Realtor:	Realtor:
Price:	Price:	Price:
Deposit:	Deposit:	Deposit:
Expiration Date/Time?	Expiration Date/Time?	Expiration Date/Time?
Cash Down: Lender Approval Letter?:	Cash Down: Lender Approval Letter?:	Cash Down: Lender Approval Letter?:
Home Warranty Amt?	Home Warranty Amt?	Home Warranty Amt?
Contingencies:	Contingencies:	Contingencies:
Closing Date:	Closing Date:	Closing Date:
Brokerage Fee: List Co: % $ XYZCo./Sale: % $	Brokerage Fee: List Co: % $ XYZCo./Sale: % $	Brokerage Fee: List Co: % $ XYZCo./Sale: % $
ESTIMATED NET to Seller before attorney fees, transfer fees, release fees, any loan payoff or other closing fees: $	*ESTIMATED NET* to Seller before attorney fees, transfer fees, release fees, any loan payoff or other closing fees: $	*ESTIMATED NET* to Seller before attorney fees, transfer fees, release fees, any loan payoff or other closing fees: $

Contract to closing

Again, this is where you can really shine, and the checklist is very similar to the buyer's checklist.

◆ In my area, most offers are contingent upon a professional home inspection of the property, which is paid for by the buyer. Be sure to notify everyone of the date and time of the inspection. I always advise my sellers to please be absent (along with their children and pets) during the inspection time, which generally takes two to three hours, depending upon the size of the home.

   If the sellers are absent from the house, the buyers can have the opportunity to feel more comfortable checking out storage areas and closets or measuring areas of rooms for their furniture, etc. It also gives them a chance to exchange questions and answers with the inspector without feeling the possible awkwardness of the sellers being in the house.

◆ Make sure that all parties have everything they need from you at least 30 days in advance. Don't become known as the "ditzy agent" who calls the attorney's office or settlement office three days prior to the closing date and expects to have everything done in time.

◆ Be prepared and confirm everything.

TAKE ACTION!

1. Prepare a Pre-Listing package, and keep at least five (5) copies ready at all times. Include before/after staging photos.
2. Prepare your "Marketing Plan" for sellers.
3. Make a checklist of all items from Listing to Contract.
4. Make a checklist of all items from Contract to Closing.

– 14 –

Negotiations

Negotiating is an art and a skill. Expertise in it comes not only from experience but also from listening, acknowledging the other party's points, and thinking before you speak. In the real estate business, there are two types of negotiations:

Negotiating on your own behalf

When you are sitting across from a potential client during a listing presentation and you are discussing and defending your commission, you are essentially negotiating your own salary.

◆ Be prepared to show your value proposition. What marketing techniques or systems do you use that are different from another agent who might charge less? In other words, why are you worth what you're charging?

◆ The "No Risk, No Reward" factor contributes to the fee structure of the real estate industry. In some areas of the country, the seller pays a retainer fee for marketing costs up front; however, most of the time the seller does not contribute up-front money toward marketing and then you are taking all the risk.

◆ What's your track record or your company's track record for the time on the market that a property takes to sell?

◆ Is your average list-to-sales price higher than your competitors?

◆ Assess all the risks. If the statistics prove that the average property is taking six months or longer to sell, then why would you take a 90-day listing and spend your energy and money if there's not a reasonable chance of it selling?

◆ Ask your seller, "If your Realtor® is so willing to reduce their fee up front, then how skilled will they be when negotiating on YOUR behalf with a prospective buyer?"

Negotiating on your seller client's behalf

There's a financial and an emotional side of every transaction, and I feel that it's the real estate professional's job to keep the emotional side balanced. When any offer comes in, I tell my sellers that they always have the final say with three choices:

1. accept the offer as is,
2. counter the offer, or
3. reject it entirely.

I then explain that the only reason to reject an offer is when we can prove that the buyers are not qualified to purchase — period! That means that the seller should not take personal offense if a low offer comes in. If the price and terms of the offer are not acceptable, then the only reasonable answer is to counter the offer with terms that the sellers can accept.

For example, a buyer's offer might request a specific closing date outside of the time that the seller hoped to close. You might want to advise the seller to counter with two different proposals:

1. Accept the existing requested date but counter with a higher price to cover the moving and storage costs for the seller.
2. Accept a lower price if the buyer will agree to a date for closing that is convenient to the seller. I have learned that everyone loves choices — they do not like to be told what to do. If explained unemotionally to all parties, then this scenario allows both parties to make a choice, and many times it becomes a win-win for all parties.

Be prepared with the most recent comparable sales in the neighborhood that support the listing price, and show them to the buyer's agent. If the comps don't support the listing price, then you will need to educate the seller again, on where the market is at that time.

Negotiating on your buyer client's behalf

When you represent a buyer, many times you will discover that they either have a preconceived notion that ALL offers should be a specific percentage lower than the list price of the property, or they might need your assistance with an initial offering price.

After the buyer has selected the home of their choice, you will need to educate them on the trends of your specific marketplace. Some areas of the country, where there are numerous foreclosures, buyers might be able to secure a price which is well below the list price. In other areas where prices have remained rather steady, or experienced a small depreciation in price, buyers will need to be shown the comparable sales which will support the list-to-sale ratios of that area.

Just as we do with sellers, it's always best to prepare a Market Analysis (CMA) to show the buyer the recent property sales, the specific features or upgrades the property has, the time-frame the property took to sell, and the difference between the list price and the final sales price.

When counseling buyers whom I represent, I generally suggest that their initial offer should be one that is not so low that it's insulting to a seller, but close enough to the market value, where a seller can't resist.

If there's a wide gap between the current market value and the seller's list price, then you may want to show the listing agent a copy of the CMA which you prepared for the buyer, to support the buyer's offer.

Remember, however, that while your job is to secure the best terms for your buyer, you don't want to offend or antagonize the listing agent or seller, or you may not receive a good response to the offer.

In summary, there's no excuse to let an agent's emotions or ego get out of control. Sellers want to sell or they would not be listed. Buyers want to purchase a property or they would not make an offer. The agents' roles are to work together toward an agreement that is acceptable to everyone.

TAKE ACTION!
1. Prepare your value proposition for a seller. What is it that you do differently from your peers?
2. Ask your mentor, or another seasoned agent, if you can listen in on a contract offer and negotiations.

15

Systems and Tools

G ood systems and tools are like a road map to get from Point A to Point B. You can identify the points on a map, but it's the roads and detours in between that can get you frazzled if you don't have a clearly mapped outline of how to get there (or, in today's world, a GPS to guide you). Just as the traveler needs a road map, every successful real estate agent needs a good database management system.

Why do you need systems and tools, you ask? To keep your client communication moving efficiently; as a benefit, you will then have personal, family, and fun time and not have to work 12-16 hour days, every day.

When I started in the real estate business in 1976, there were no high-tech database systems, there was no email, and even home computers didn't exist. My database management system consisted of a box of 3x5 index cards arranged alphabetically by name with all my contact notes scribbled on the front, back, and even multiple cards stapled together.

How times have changed! Today's high-tech database management systems give you the opportunity to access contacts and send notes and newsletters with the touch of a few keys.

What's a system? What's a tool?

A *system* is a documented way of completing tasks that need to be done on a regular basis. A *tool* is one of the items that needs to be completed for the system to work. For example, the system could be your monthly newsletter, and the tool could be the statistics that are needed in order to complete the newsletter and get it ready for mailing.

I have used an electronic database system for many years and feel that I could not do business without it; these days it also includes my daily calendar, which synchronizes with my smart phone. Here's a sample of how my database is set up:

◆ Calendar: My electronic calendar contains both business and personal appointments so that everything is in one place. It also allows me to enter regularly occurring meetings or appointments, such as our weekly company meetings, as recurring events. The system can also be set up to send me an email reminder about specific deadlines and other items.

◆ Database of contacts: It is crucial to keep all information on each contact in one place. The database I use allows me to establish contact "types" so that when I want to view all past clients who have purchased and sold through me, it can be done in one easy step.

Some of the contact types I use are:

◇ The source: Where they came from — sign call, ad call, personal referral, Internet marketing, etc.

◇ Buyer or Seller prospect

◇ If they are a buyer, are they an A, B, C or D buyer — i.e., ready to buy within 3 months, within 1-2 years, need to sell a home first, or just looking. This makes it easy to search, for instance for all of your A buyers when a great property has just come on the market.

◇ Year they first contacted me

◇ Year they closed on a property

By using contact types, it also helps me to prepare a year-end chart of where my business comes from and what's the best ROI (return on my investment). I can search for how many buyers and sellers actually closed in any year and where they came from. I can then prepare a simple

Excel chart showing percentages of each source of business. (If you're not familiar with the Excel program, then find someone who is, and pay them to set up your template. Once that is complete, you only need to insert the data into the different fields, and that's very easy.)

Sometimes, I show a few years of these charts to sellers when they ask me how many newspaper ads and "Homes Magazine" ads I plan to do for them. Though I could prove that a small percentage of my sales resulted from paper ads and open houses in the early 2000s, my most recent year charts show that those sources of business have fallen off dramatically, and that Internet marketing and personal referrals have provided a much better ROI than paper ads. I also ask my sellers, "If you owned a business, would you spend money where there was no return on your investment?" Most of the time they agree, and this chart supports my marketing plans.

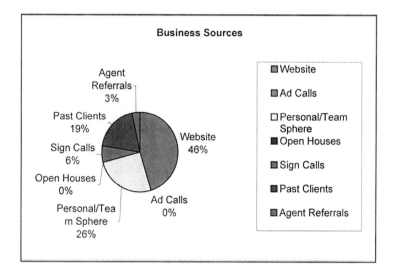

◆ Action plans for listings: This is a checklist for who does what and when. It consists of a series of tasks, starting with preparing the initial Pre-Listing Package, and includes taking photos, preparing virtual tours or videos, all the way to the contract. If you have a team, then tasks can be separated and assigned to different team members. I have another action plan for contract to closing.

◆ Action plans for buyer leads: This is a series of reminders for emails, letters, and phone calls to prospective buyers to keep your name in front of them until they're ready to buy.

One of the biggest mistakes some agents make is to disregard the buyer or seller prospect who is not ready to do business at the moment. They represent a great opportunity, and it's important to keep in communication with them; a good database and action plans are the tools to do it! Why? I've had buyers call me to say that they have been receiving my newsletters and communications for the previous three years and that they are now ready to buy. Since I've been the only agent who has stayed in touch, they've decided to contact me.

These action plans can be set up so that you have a daily reminder of activities to do, relating to each prospect.

♦ Don't forget to add each and every email address to your newsletter and mailing lists. Make certain that you offer a place for prospects to unsubscribe, if they so choose.

The following pages are sample Action Plans from my database program:

Action Plan for Leads

	Activity	Description	Day	Assigned To	Date Completed
1.	Email	Reply to prospect with info requested	1		
2.	To-do	Mail Relocation Pkg. (if requested)	1		
3.	Call	Call prospect	1		
4.	To-do	Enter prospect & all info into database	2		
5.	Email	Letter #1	10		
6.	Email	Letter #2	20		
7.	Mail	Letter #3	30		
8.	Email	Letter #4	40		
9.	Call	Touch-Call from Buyer Specialist	50		
10.	Email	Letter #5	70		
11.	To-do	Handwritten note to prospect	90		
12.	Email	Letter #6	110		
13.	Email	Letter #7	130		
14.	Email	Letter #8	150		
15.	Mail	Letter #9	170		
16.	Email	Letter #10	190		
17.	Email	Letter #11	210		
18.	Call	Touch-Call from Buyer Specialist	220		
19.	To-do	Handwritten note following call	225		
20.	Email	Letter #12	250		

Action Plan for Listings

	Activity	Description	Assigned To	Date Completed
1.	To-do	Prepare Listing Package for Sellers		
2.	To-do	Deliver Pre-List package to Sellers		
3.	To-do	Listing Appointment		
4.	To-do/Call	Measure house (confirm appt. w/sellers)		
5.	To-do/Call	Take Photos for tour (confirm appt. w/sellers)		
6.	To-do	Upload photos to DropBox		
7.	To-do	Lockbox & Sign up		
8.	To-do	Prepare Brochure		
9.	To-do	Review paperwork for initials, signature, etc.		
10.	To-do	Post on Bulletin board		
11.	To-do	Create VTour & upload to all websites and MLS		
12.	To-do	MLS Entry w/Photos, disclosures, brochure		
13.	To-do	Enter into Homefeedback		
14.	To-do	Prepare listing transmittal sheet		
15.	To-do	Copy of MLS sheet to Front Desk		
16.	To-do	Order Home Warranty (if applicable)		
17.	To-do	Give all originals to Office for main file		
18.	To-do	Enter listing into TP database program		
19.	To-do	Mail "Thank you" to seller with copies		
20.	To-do/Call	Schedule Office previews (confirm w/sellers)		
21.	To-do/Call	Schedule Broker previews (confirm w/sellers)		
22.	To-do	Scan and send listing link to Team Leader		
23.	To-do	Email Flyer announcement to Board Realtor group		
24.	To-do	Email blast to database and past clients		
25.	To-do	Email Seller updates from VTour and Realtor.com		
26.	To-do	Prepare 30-day Seller Report		
27.	To-do/Call	Review Market Position with seller		
28.	To-do	Prepare 60-day Seller Report		
29.	To-do/Call	Review Market Position with seller		
30.	To-do	Prepare 90-day Seller Report		
31.	To-do/Call	Review Market Position with seller		
32.	To-do	Check Renewal date and prepare extension		
33.	To-do	Extend listing in MLS and TP action plans		
***	To-do	ALL Price changes: MLS, websites, R.com, HFB, etc.		
***	To-do/Call	Schedule Open House (if applicable & confirm w/seller)		

Action Plan – Buyer Closings

	Activity	Description	Assigned To	Date Completed
1.	To-do	Professional Services Disclosure complete		
2.	To-do	Buyer Receipt of HOA/Condo/PUD documents		
3.	To-do	Offer Presented/Accepted/Signed		
4.	To-do	Earnest Money check rec'd from Buyer		
5.	To-do	Earnest Money check to listing firm		
6.	To-do	Give all signed paperwork to Team Assistant		
7.	To-do	Review paperwork for sigs and initials		
8.	To-do	Prepare transmittal sheet & give to office		
9.	To-do/Eml	Mail copy contract to Lender		
10.	To-do/Call	Order home inspection (confirm w/all parties)		
11.	To-do/Eml	Order home warranty (if applicable)		
12.	To-do	Order septic inspection if necessary		
13.	To-do	Send Buyer Letter #1 (introduce closing coordinator)		
14.	To-do	Enter status on Bulletin board		
15.	To-do	Send Loan Pre-Approval letter (if applicable)		
16.	To-do	Enter all info into TP database		
17.	To-do	Check dates on Contract with Closing Plan		
18.	To-do	Enter closing date on TP Calendar w/reminder		
19.	To-do/Call	Call Buyer: closing by mail? Attending?/POA?		
20.	To-do/Eml	Prepare form & send instructions to closing attorney		
21.	To-do	Scan all docs and email info to Team Leader		
22.	To-do	Order survey & site elevation (if applicable)		
23.	To-do	Order Pest Inspection (confirm with LA)		
24.	To-do	Home Inspection results received?		
25.	To-do	Repair Request: send to Buyers and Seller's agent		
26.	To-do/Call	Buyer contacted: Insurance company?		
27.	To-do/Call	Check w/lender on appraisal		
29.	To-do/Call	Repair Request received back from sellers?		
29.	To-do	All paperwork turned into office?		
30.	To-do	Notify LA: do not turn off utilities		
31.	To-do/Eml	Utility company info to buyer		
32.	To-do	Final Loan approval letter to seller's agent		
33.	To-do/Eml	Confirm closing date and time w/all parties		
34.	To-do/Eml	Schedule walk-thru (confirm with all parties)		
35.	To-do/Eml	Request copy of HUD from closing office		
36.	To-do/Call	Review HUD with buyers		
37.	To-do	Prepare closing gift for buyers		
38.	To-do/Call	Remind buyers: Certified funds		
39.	To-do/Call	Check status of loan package from lender		
40.	To-do/Call	Confirm w/listing agent that repairs are complete		
41.	To-do	Attend closing		
42.	To-do	Arrange pick-up commission check		
43.	To-do	Check and HUD to office		
44.	To-do	Scan HUD to contract file and email to Team Leader		
45.	To-do	Update Top Producer & add to follow up program		
46.	To-do	Update Anniversary Card list		
47.	To-do	Prepare & send thank-you and Survey to buyers		
48.	To-do	Update buyer's email address and add to database		
49.	To-do/Call	Call buyers for Follow-up		

Action Plan – Seller Closings

	Activity	Description	Assigned To	Date Completed
1.	To-do	Offer Presented & Accepted		
2.	To-do	Prepare transmittal sheet (EMD check & docs to office)		
3.	To-do	Review paperwork for sigs and initials		
4.	To-do	Enter all info into TP database & change to Pending		
5.	To-do	Check dates on Contract with Closing Plan		
6.	To-do	Enter closing date on TP Calendar w/reminder		
7.	To-do	Enter status on Bulletin board		
8.	To-do	Pending Rider on sign		
9.	To-do	Pend in MLS, and all websites		
10.	To-do	Home Warranty?		
11.	To-do	Mail signed copies to all parties		
12.	To-do/Eml	Congratulations letter to seller		
13.	To-do/Eml	Thank you note to selling agent		
14.	To-do	Scan all docs and email link to Team Leader		
15.	To-do/Call	Call Sellers: attend closing? Arrange proceeds?		
16.	To-do/Eml	Prepare form & send instructions to closing attorney		
17.	To-do/Eml	Home Inspection: confirm date/time w/all parties		
18.	To-do/Call	Review Inspection Report w/sellers		
19.	To-do/Eml	Repair Request signed by all parties?		
20.	To-do/Call	Buyer Loan commitment letter?		
21.	To-do/Call	Check w/buyer's agent on appraisal		
22.	To-do/Eml	Letter to Seller with closing information.		
23.	To-do	All paperwork turned into office?		
24.	To-do/Call	Remind sellers to change utilities		
25.	To-do/Call	Final Loan approval letter from buyer's agent?		
26.	To-do/Call	Confirm closing date and time w/all parties		
27.	To-do/Call	Call buyer's agent – Walk-thru date and time?		
29.	To-do	Repairs completed?		
29.	To-do/Eml	Request copy of HUD from closing office		
30.	To-do/Call	Review HUD with Sellers		
31.	To-do	Prepare closing gift for sellers		
32.	To-do/Eml	Check status of loan package from lender		
33.	To-do	Attend Closing		
34.	To-do	Arrange pick-up commission check		
35.	To-do	Check and HUD to office		
36.	To-do	Scan HUD to contract file and email to Team Leader		
37.	To-do	Take sign and lockbox down		
38.	To-do	Update Top Producer & add to follow up program		
39.	To-do	Update Anniversary Card list		
40.	To-do	Prepare & send thank-you and Survey to Sellers		
41.	To-do	Update Seller's email address and add to database		
42.	To-do	Call Sellers for Follow-up		

TAKE ACTION!

1. Enter the names of all your contacts and leads into your database management system.
2. Assign them a contact type and add any notes that may be pertinent.
3. Assign an Action Plan.

16

Internet Marketing

"Technology won't replace agents.
Agents who know how to maximize technology
will replace agents." — *Burke Smith*

Internet marketing has become one of my favorite tools. Many of my colleagues and peers consider me "tech-savvy" in this area, but it wasn't always that way.

I'd like to share a short story of how I was introduced to Internet marketing. When I moved to North Carolina after 20 years of a successful business in the Northern Virginia area, I possessed the experience and some systems for a successful business. However, I had no contacts and no sphere in my new location, and I felt like I was starting from scratch.

The average sales price of a house in Northern Virginia in 1996 was about $250,000. At about the same time, in the New Bern, North Carolina area, the average sales price was about $80,000. What a difference! I felt like I was starting all over again as a rookie agent; I was also in a much lower price range than I was accustomed to. After a lot of soul-searching, I put my bruised ego on the shelf and realized that I had to get back to basics. At that time in the mid-90s, my daughter was a college student. Technology and computer science were not her major, but she discovered that she loved website design; she did lots of research on it, and it ended up becoming her hobby.

One weekend when she was visiting, and I was complaining about lack of business in this new area, my daughter suggested that I needed a website.

I thought, Why not! After all, we had moved to coastal eastern North Carolina where the climate was more to our liking, where there was less congestion than the larger city, and where we could enjoy more outdoor activities year round, like golf and boating. I was sure that there were many other people in different parts of the country, especially the Northeast, who might want to consider the same type of relocation. I decided that this would be my niche: gearing the website toward relocating buyers, the retirees and semi-retirees, who desired a less hectic lifestyle.

So, with my daughter's help, I started putting together my own personal real estate website from scratch. One of the first things that I did was go online and research numerous sites from agents all over the country. I placed myself in the consumer seat and asked, "What would I like to see online if I were considering a move to a new location?"

My website

In my research, I found that too many agent sites were generic in content. That is, they were created by professional web masters or design groups, and they used the same template. They all had the same bells and whistles (albeit in different colors) and only offered generic reports, along with general information on purchasing real estate. I came to the conclusion that, in order to be effective, my website needed to have local content, so the consumer could take a tour of my city and marketplace and see what we had to offer.

To help give my website the local content, I took a lot of photos of local attractions myself — places that I thought people would be interested in viewing about our marketplace. I still carry a digital camera in my car, and even today I will stop and take a photo of something that's been updated or a new attraction that I feel would be of interest to a consumer and add it to the website.

At the time, a neighbor was an IT manager for a large company and offered to help. I provided the information, my daughter set up the categories and design, and he tweaked the final product and got it online.

That was the beginning of my Internet marketing, and I read everything I could find about how to get and keep good rankings in the search engines. You cannot put a website into cyberspace and leave it there, expecting to receive inquiries. I even hired an SEO (Search Engine Optimization) specialist to review the site and add the proper coding that it needed in order to be found quickly by the search engines on the different sites

Today, there are numerous customizable template websites that will work just as well as and are much easier to maintain than the original, custom HTML coding. However, content is still key. People want to see photos and tours, and they want information: What's the area like? Show me several photos. Show me a slide presentation on the city/town and what it has to offer, or show me a video. Tell me about the schools, and where do I go to find more information? Show me photos of homes for sale, and tell me about them.

The following is a list of the different page links that make a winning real estate site. Most of the template sites allow you to add information, so you can create similar pages with your customizable template site:

- Home page, with a link for Best Buys and for Free Relocation Packages
- Link to Search our local MLS on the front page
- About Dianne & Team
- My listings, including 15 photos, complete descriptions, virtual tours, and a PDF brochure on properties that the consumer can print out.

- Historic New Bern, NC, and subcategories:
  - ◇ New Bern tour
  - ◇ View neighborhoods
  - ◇ New Bern attractions
  - ◇ New Bern history
- Things to Do in New Bern:
  - ◇ Golfing
  - ◇ Boating
  - ◇ NC beaches
  - ◇ New Bern Mum Fest
  - ◇ Trolley tours
  - ◇ Art galleries
  - ◇ Restaurants and dining
  - ◇ For kids
- New Bern Facts and Information
  - ◇ Medical/Healthcare
  - ◇ Travel/Maps
  - ◇ Government/Taxes
  - ◇ Schools
  - ◇ Worship
- Hotels/Bed & Breakfasts
- Tips for Buyers (customized)
- Tips for Sellers (customized)
- New Bern Links (to all local TV, radio, etc.)
- North Carolina Links (sports, attractions, and official state site)
- "Going Green" — tips and website links on energy efficiency and environmentally friendly ways to upgrade and update your home.

What's most important for your website?

Here are some tips on what to focus on in your website:

◆ Content is key and it's extremely important. You need to have current information on your site and review and update it several times a year. If your listings page is updated on a regular basis, that also helps with search engine placement.

◆ Lots of photos and virtual tours or videos. Consumers want to see what a property looks like, both inside and out. Give them a great tour of the property, and provide all information you can about property associations, etc., but make sure it is current information. Remember: when consumers see only one photo for a listing, they skip over it.

> ➔ *TIP: On all of my websites, I leave the sold properties on the site for about one year, with a clear label saying "sold." The consumer then has a good idea of what homes are selling for.*

◊ Response time is critical. When a consumer finds your site on the Internet and sends an inquiry about a property or your area, it is extremely important to reply as soon as possible, or at least within four hours, or you will lose them to the next website.

◇ I have an auto-responder set up to acknowledge that we have received their
request and we will be in touch with
them shortly with information they requested.

◇ Then I customize a series of standard
paragraphs to the prospect, and these are
emailed as soon as possible. (See examples
on next page.)

Remember the old cliché: "The early bird
gets the worm!"

My website has received several comments over
the last 13 years, especially when I have asked for feedback about how they found me and what made them
select me:

♦ "I like your site because it gives me lots of
good detailed information on the New Bern
area!"

♦ "I like your site because you don't have a
window that pops up and insists that I sign
in before I can view the site or view home
listings."

♦ "We come back to your site often, because
it's easy to navigate."

Website Auto-Responder:

Hi (Name captured from Reply form)

Thank you for visiting my web site! I hope that you found the information about the New Bern area informative.

This auto responder confirms that your message was received and that I will personally be in touch with you shortly, regarding the information that you requested.

Thanks again for stopping by, and please come again soon!

P.S. You can search ALL active listings in our MLS by clicking on the following link:
http://www.SearchNewBernHomes.com

Best Regards,

My signature lines.

"Personalized" Standard Reply:

Hi, (FIRST NAMES)

I received your request, and a Relocation Package on the New Bern, NC area will be in the mail to you shortly. Thank you for contacting us!

Through our Multiple Listing Service, w can show you "New" and "Resale" properties listed by ANY real estate company. In addition, we also work with all of the developers of communities selling land and lots, along with numerous new-home Builders.

We assist many people from all over the country who are considering relocating to the New Bern area, and who contact us from my Web Site. We work with people exclusively as a Buyer's agent under a written agreement. If you are not currently under a written agreement with another Realtor®, we would be happy to assist you! The following link will explain how licensed Realtors in North Carolina can work with you and represent you. Please feel free to contact us if you have any questions about this brochure.
http://www.ddunn.com/files/WorkingWithREAgents-Brochure.pdf

You can also view ALL current property listings in New Bern (much more up-to-the-minute information than the Realtor.com site or other real estate sites).
Just go to: http://NewBernHomeSearch.com and select your desired criteria!

Please give us enough advance notice of the dates that you will be planning a trip here, since many people schedule appointments several weeks in advance. We can then coordinate both of our schedules, so that we can show you the New Bern area and some properties or homes in the price range that you prefer.

We look forward to hearing from you!

Best Regards,

Buy your own domain name

This is critical. You need to own your own domain (and email address) so that the site stays with you. While you may be very happy with your existing company, you don't know where you will be in a few years. You don't want to pay for something that you cannot take with you, whether you transfer to another firm or start your own.

Purchase your own domain name so that it will include several email addresses. For example, www. NewBernHomes.com is my main domain name, and I have email addresses for general information as well as for me and each member of my team: DDunn@ NewBernHomes.com or Info@NewBernHomes.com and the team names.

I'll say it again: Content is key, and continuous updates drive more traffic to your site through the main search engines. Regular updates can be your listings page, where you change their status from For Sale to Pending to Sold. If you are in a slow market in which listings are taking a long time to sell, make sure to update your photos. If it's summer and your website (or your MLS) shows an outdated photo of the house with snow or brown grass from the winter, the property looks stale, and buyers will try to low-ball a price.

There are now several virtual tour packages that you can use to produce a tour of each property. I've used VisualTours.com for several years. That company charges a fairly inexpensive monthly fee for unlimited tours (homes, neighborhoods, etc.).

I discovered the VisualTour® program and many other forms of technology when I attended a real estate technology seminar in the late 1990s. The national speaker was a CRS Instructor who happened to be an old friend of mine from the Northern Virginia area, Allen Hainge. Since then, Allen has been the founder of the CyberStars™ group and has been on the national circuit teaching CRS and GRI courses, in addition to publishing several books on real estate technology.

After attending this seminar and seeing Allen again, I was honored that he asked me to join the exclusive CyberStars™ group, which at the time had about 40 agents all over the country. He invites agents who are experienced in production, have a customized website, use current technology in their business, and are willing to share their ideas with others in the group. Only one agent is selected from a marketplace area, and there are currently about 250 CyberStars™ around the country and Canada.

I came back from that seminar charged with new ideas, and have been an active member ever since. Allen Hainge and the CyberStars™ have helped me tremendously by sharing ways to work smarter — not harder — and by using simple technology in my everyday business.

You don't have to be a tech-geek to understand and use some of the basic technology that's available for agents today. The following are a few of the tech gadgets that I could not live without:

◆ A Smartphone that synchs to my database to keep me up-to-date at all times.

◆ A laptop computer — I've had several, including a tablet in which the screen flattens and allows you to draw, sign, and send out information. However, I found it very heavy since it included a built-in DVD drive that I did not use very, so I recently purchased one without the DVD drive. It weighs under two pounds, and is very easy to carry with me and use.

◆ Fujitsu ScanSnap — small, one-button compact scanner that scans about 20 pages per minute into PDF format, right into my computer.

◆ E-Fax or any type of fax-to-email, so that all faxes come directly to my email in PDF format. This saves a lot of time and doesn't require replenishing paper to an old-style fax machine.

◆ Digital camera with wide-angle lens to take photos of entire rooms.

◆ TopProducer® database management system.

- An air card with unlimited Internet connection time. This small device connects the laptop to the Internet through the computer's USB port. Mine was purchased through my cell phone carrier for a flat monthly fee. I find it invaluable to have Internet connection most any where.

- Snag-it.com — allows you to capture small images or large website pages with a simple click, and save them to your computer as a PDF or jpg format.

- Flash or thumb drives — these are small, portable storage gadgets that can hold at least 16 Gigabytes worth of information (1 byte = 1 character, 1 Gigabyte = 1 million characters). These allow me to carry information on me so I don't have to work on a particular computer; I can prepare information on one computer, transfer it to my thumb drive, and then transfer it to a different computer to continue working.

Social media

While many originally believed that blogging and social media platforms such as Facebook™, Twitter™, etc. were just typical fads, some surveys and statistics today are proving that agents are increasing their business by using these marketing platforms. They offer a powerful opportunity to brand ourselves and our real estate business, and to show that we are knowledgeable and current with what's happening in the marketplace.

There's a big difference between posting the basics, such as where you're going today, or what you had to eat last night, and posting valuable information that everyone can use. The following are some items to consider:

- Post a link to an interesting article you read and want to share — perhaps an article about how to reduce energy and convert your home to "going green."
- Post new property listings with links to photos and information on why they're such a great buy.
- Post items of interest about your city/town, i.e. restaurants, theatres, museums, and other types of places and activities that consumers might enjoy.

Be very careful what you say in your blogging or on your Facebook or Twitter site, since it's published for everyone to see, and you want to ensure that what you say is either inspiring or useful and professional.

> **_TAKE ACTION!_**
> 1. Research website providers and select the best one for you.
> 2. Purchase your own domain name.
> 3. Set aside time each day to update and add "local content" until you have the website completed.
> 4. Prepare your auto-response.
> 5. Prepare your "standard, customized" paragraphs for quick responses to email inquiries.
> 6. Review tech tools and select the best ones for you and your budget.

17

Assistants? Why, When, and How to Hire Them

Whether you are a solo agent or aspire to a team concept, as your business grows, you may not be able to do it all by yourself. There are several reasons you may want to hire help:

- To get relief from all the necessary paperwork
- To gain more face-to-face time with buyers and sellers
- To enjoy more personal time with family and friends

Two types of assistants

1. A personal assistant who works in your office.
2. A virtual assistant and/or team, who works from their own office which can be located anywhere in the country.

Over the years, I have witnessed many agents who have hired personal assistants and had no clue about how to use them efficiently. After spending money and time on training, the agents have ended up more flustered than when they worked solo.

This chapter is more extensive than some of the other ones because I want to help you benefit from my personal successes and failures with hired help. Before you hire anyone, remember that the assistant pain-or-pleasure experience has everything to do with YOUR preparation.

"So, what exactly do you want me to do?"

This well might be the first question from your new assistant.

Answer:

"Well, I want you to take over many of the administrative tasks of my business, and here's the manual on how to do that.

I also want you to monitor the marketing of my listings, and here's my checklist. In addition, I want you to handle all of my closings — this is how each step is done in chronological order.

Here is what your perfect day, week, and month will look like. We'll have morning office meetings once a week to make sure you are on schedule, that all priorities are being handled, and that we, as a team, are meeting our pre-determined goals."

Are you ready to say this to your assistant?

The following are some suggestions and guidelines:

> → *TIP: If you aspire to grow a team and have Buyer Specialists and Listing Specialists working with you, I suggest that you have only your photo on the sign, along with your team name, etc. Team members change, but you do not, and it's very expensive to have new signs made each time there is a change in personnel.*

Getting things ready

Start by giving some assistant responsibilities to your family

◆ Do you have a teenager who would wash the car and run errands for less than an assistant costs?

◆ The same goes for your spouse; can he/she keep track of your expenses with a computer program, or install or take down your signs?

◆ Broker-paid staffers are sometimes available for direct mailings or creating listing brochures. Before you pay an assistant, make sure that all your inexpensive or free resources are utilized. Don't use your Assistant as a "gofer!"

Identify your assistant's main responsibilities

◆ Do you need someone to manage the day-to-day administrative operations of your business? i.e. answer the phone, check mail and email, prepare your updates to sellers, prepare for your open houses, manage all the details from contract to closing?

OR

◆ Do you need someone who will lead-generate for new business for you?

It's very difficult for one person to handle both responsibilities efficiently if your business is very active. So, after you make this decision, you can proceed with your planning. I have used a combination of both a personal assistant and a virtual assistant team to split the responsibilities of managing my business. The lead-generation part had been handled by me until I grew my team to include a listing specialist and buyer specialists — then lead-generation responsibility was delegated to them.

Checklist and "manualize" everything

◆ Start with your first project that you do each day. Is it opening your email first? Is it checking your messages? Is it checking your MLS update to see what new properties are on the market for your prospect list?

◆ Do you hold Open Houses? Then write down everything that you do (or should be doing) to plan for a successful Open House. Start with the phone call to the sellers to be ready, preparing neighborhood announcements to send out, making copies of the property brochures, having enough personal brochures and business cards at the house, refreshments, sign-in sheets, etc., as well as the procedures for following up with the people you meet at the Open House. If you do a free drawing for people who attend, include information on how that is handled as well.

◆ What is your process for entering leads into your database management system, and assigning contact types and an action plan?

◆ Define the process from contract to closing and list each step in chronological order. Who do they contact first? Who receives copies and when? Which are the critical dates that they need reminders for?

Whatever it is, write down detailed instructions on what you do and how you do it, including your computer IDs and passwords (for on-line work). You can't expect your new assistant to be trained through osmosis.

Define the manual

◆ Start with a three-ring binder and plenty of plastic, protective covers for each page of the manual. Use labels to separate the different tasks.

◆ What are the projects that need to be completed on a daily basis? A weekly basis? A monthly basis? An annual basis? Put these in the manual and classify them by their frequency. For example:

Daily:	Handle all mail
	Handle all email inquiries
	Handle closing details
Weekly:	Check for feedback on
	listing, showings
	Check office supplies
Monthly:	Update, and send your
	newsletters
	Update any special neighborhood
	reports needed for CMAs and
	mailings

◆ Do you struggle with last-minute deadlines every year, trying to get all of your files together for submission to your Board of REALTORS® for annual awards or for your tax preparation? Your assistant can keep your report updated on a regular basis, once you write down the process of where to find the material, and provide the correct form to record it. This, too, goes in the manual.

◆ If you want your assistant to act as your Client-Care Manager, then you'll need a good real estate database management program, as mentioned in Chapter 8 to keep track of every step, from contract to closing. A chronological list of activities and time frame should also be included in this manual.

Everything in real estate starts with a plan!

Whether you, your assistant, or your Listing/Buyer Specialist handle lead-generation, you will need to identify the demographics of prospecting, and who will most likely bring in more business to you (your sphere of influence, your website leads, FSBO's (For Sale by Owner), absentee owners, expired listings. These people are your "lead generators," whether it's generating leads for buyers or for seller listings.

The next step is figuring out an impressive delivery system (phone, mail, email, and/or website). Written letter samples, scripts, and other guidelines and tips need to be written down. Then you'll need a written follow-up plan on how to handle these new leads. All this paper-work necessitates that you, the agent, have to have done those procedures first, so that you will know how to explain them to your Assistant.

This procedure forces you to write an efficient manual on proactive "lead generation" for sellers, if that is going to be one of the Assistant's tasks or the responsibility of your Listing/Buyer Specialist.

Outsourcing to a VA (Virtual Assistant)

Consider outsourcing some of your projects to a virtual assistant (VA). Whether it is research work for monthly statistics, direct mail, or website maintenance, sometimes it can be better delegated for less money to a professional VA.

- I had my VA and her team design a template for monthly postcards. While one side of the card remains constant, (i.e., information about my services and how to contact me), the back side shows "Just listed" and "Just sold" properties for that month. Whenever I have a new listing, my VA adds the photo and information very easily and has a service print and mail them to a specific neighborhood that I designate. I also have copies sent to past clients as part of my monthly "keeping-in-touch" system.
- My VA also performs tasks like keeping an Absorption Rate Chart updated each month, researching and preparing the

statistics, and sending out the monthly e-newsletter. They keep track of their time in 15-minute intervals, and send me a monthly bill by email. I pay it with credit card using PayPal and everything works smoothly. I have had the same virtual assistant team for seven years and have been very pleased.

Help and assistance comes from many forms

◆ Get your sellers involved in the process. In the Pre-Listing Package that is emailed or delivered to my sellers, I always ask them to have a few documents ready, along with two house keys, when we meet at the presentation. If these items are ready at the time of the presentation, I'm delighted with the expectation of a new listing, and the satisfaction of knowing that my Assistant has more time to focus on her responsibilities, instead of running around collecting documents and making duplicate keys.

◆ When I used brochure boxes on my real estate signs, my sellers were responsible for keeping the brochure box filled with copies, and contacting my Assistant when copies got low. Taking this task one step further, consider subscribing to an on-line service where "everyone" involved in a transaction can go online to report the progress, send email requests, or check the status of the transaction. Assistants can follow up with feedback, and everyone involved has an update! Those systems, once again, keep the sellers involved and will keep your Assistant focused on his/her main responsibilities.

Regarding yard sign brochure boxes — I used them for years and then stopped in the fall of 2007. Why? I realized that during a downturn in our market, homes were taking much longer to sell than 30-60 days. Boxes got broken, colored brochure copies were ruined when it rained, and the cost and effort to keep these boxes in place and in good condition was getting out of hand. The biggest eye-opener for me was that we were not receiving any calls — rather, we were giving out all the information about the property on the brochure, so there was no need for the prospect to call us.

As a replacement for the brochure boxes, I ordered large sign riders that connected to my signs. They were white with bright red lettering that said, "Photos, Tours, Brochure...NewBernHomes.com." This was an effort to drive more inquiries to my website. I also had my web designer add a link where we could upload the entire brochure in PDF format, and the consumer could print out any listing.

There is an old saying, "If it ain't broke, then don't fix it." However, in this case I felt that this system was broken, and I needed a replacement to bring in more live leads. When explained properly to my sellers, only about 1 out of 15 at the time objected and wanted to keep the brochure box. With that particular seller, we came to an agreement that I would leave the box for one more month before going to the new sign rider. (It happened that the property went under contract during that period, and I didn't need to replace it.)

After the sign riders replaced the brochure boxes, I discovered through my website statistics that more consumers were viewing my website, which meant more new leads. In addition, I saved a lot of time and expense by eliminating the brochure boxes and copying costs!

Technology-related preparations

◆ Do you have a good digital camera for house photos? Is the computer that your assistant will be using a relic? Think about efficiency, and how valuable time really is!

◆ Is your office equipment nearby so that your assistant does not have to waste time using the main office equipment and perhaps waiting in line? If not, then buy your own and keep it in your office. Better yet, subscribe to an e-fax service where all faxes are sent to your designated email address in the form of PDFs.

+ If you are using virtual tours of your property listings, you need a good graphics program that can upload and edit photos for listings, or upload and email them to your VA. There are many programs available, and it's just a matter of which one you prefer and which is easy and cost effective for the job.

+ A program that is well worth the money is Adobe® Acrobat® Pro (the full program, not just the free Reader download). I use it, and my assistant uses it, to convert all of our typed contracts and listing forms to a PDF format. While a Word document can also be emailed, we use the PDF format so that it's locked and the wording can't be changed. Clients can download a free version of the Adobe Reader so they can open the attachments sent. (To assist customers and clients with downloading the Adobe Reader, I have included a small icon after the signature line of my emails that links them to the Adobe program site for the free Reader.)

+ With all of the computer viruses going around, and the warnings about opening up attachments, I sometimes upload completed real estate forms, flyers, and other information to my website server and send my clients a one-line link to download the documents. (Setting this up on your server is a subject beyond the scope of this book, so check with your tech-guru if you want to learn more about uploading documents to your server.)

◆ Are you using a high-speed Internet connection? You should be. Don't expect a proficient Assistant to work with the dated "dial-up" service.

Is everything ready?

◆ Do you have the space, desk and equipment set up?

◆ Do you have your broker's approval?

◆ Do you have your accountant's approval?

◆ How about your payroll account? Assistants are employees, and to avoid issues with the IRS, you should be paying them as employees and providing a W-2 at the end of the year. If you pay them "under the table" or as an independent contractor, then expect a call from your local IRS agent with possible fines and penalties. Assistants are not independent contractors, no matter what we think!

◆ Do they need a license? It depends on what types of work they are doing. In my state, anyone who is providing real estate information to the public needs a license. Check with your state's Real Estate Commission or Board.

My first assistant came to me through my "sphere of influence" on a personal recommendation. Fortunately for me, it all worked out fine, but I was not nearly as organized with my manual as I am today. When she moved on, after two years, it encouraged me to reorganize our checklists and guidelines into a manual for my new assistant.

Hiring the assistant

- ◆ The ad:
  - ◊ In searching for an assistant, I gave lots of thought to preparing an ad for our local newspaper, giving no names, phone number, or mailing address for replies. I requested that resumes be attached and sent to an email address set up specifically for this purpose. (If the candidate cannot prepare a professional-looking resume or doesn't know how to email, then this is not likely a person I want to interview.)
  - ◊ I received numerous excellent resumes from women and men alike. I scrutinized them carefully for past or current jobs where "people skills" were important. In addition, I wanted someone who was computer-savvy enough so that I didn't need to spend a lot of my time training them on the basics.
  - ◊ I feel strongly that most people will do a better job if they are motivated and have

an incentive to do so. My ad also included the term "profit-sharing." In addition to the regular hourly rate/salary, I decided to reward my new assistant with a bonus for each closing that she handled from start to finish. Bonuses might be anywhere from $50 to $100 per transaction, depending upon how much work is involved in reaching a smooth closing. Since I had more than 60 closings in the prior year working as a solo-agent, that additional compensation held out the prospect of a nice bonus for my assistant!

- ◆ The interview
  - ◇ It is important to devise your questions like "where do you see yourself in two years?" If the answer is "moving back to Florida," maybe you may not want to invest the resources for training this person. If their answer is "being the best real estate agent in the world," you may not want to spend your efforts training your "future competition," unless that person becomes part of your sales team.
  - ◇ Ask question after question until you get a feel that this person would advance the systems and tools you have mentioned in the manual, and will be happy to help you grow your business.

◇ Once the assistant is hired, identify a 90-day trial period (best to have it in writing, signed by both of you). You should spell out definitive guidelines in order for the assistant to do the best job.

◇ After interviewing several people, I realized that many of them had numerous local contacts and other spheres of influence. Therefore, I suggested that my new assistant obtain her real estate license so that I would be able to pay her a 25 percent referral fee for each seller or buyer that she referred to me. I agreed to pay for the license education course and the annual mandatory education courses in order to keep her license active.

Note: Some of these general guidelines have been inspired by an article by Walter Sanford, national training and coach (www.Walter-Sanford.com).

TAKE ACTION!

1. Review your workload, and decide whether you need help.
2. Decide on how much you can afford to pay.
3. Start preparing your assistant's manual, and follow the steps for hiring a good one.

– 18 –

Budgeting Your Time and Money for a Good Life!

Planning your business budget

There's an old cliché: "You need to spend money to make money." Well, part of that's true; however, you don't need to spend a fortune to keep your name and branding in front of consumers.

- Start with a plan. How much money can you afford to invest in your business? Break it down to a monthly dollar amount.
- Consider the regular or continuing expenses that you will have. Will you be paying for the following, or will your company pay?
  ◇ Advertising and marketing (print or Internet ads)
  ◇ Personal website design and maintenance
  ◇ Signs and directional arrows

◇ Computers, including laptops and pro-
grams
◇ Office supplies and business cards
◇ Long-distance phone calls
◇ MLS monthly fees
◇ Auto expenses and gas
◇ Federal, FICA and state employment taxes
◇ Annual association dues to your local,
state, and national boards
◇ Lockboxes
◇ Personal assistant/staff salaries
◇ Annual license renewal fees
◇ Personal Error and Omissions Insurance
◇ Health/Medical insurance
◇ IRA or retirement fund

◆ After you have a dollar figure associated with
each category, you will have a better idea of
how to budget each month. Treat it like a
house-hold budget, if you have a good one.

Remember, as Independent Contractors, we receive "gross" commission
checks, and it's easy to think that we have
all that money to spend on ourselves.
STOP RIGHT THERE. Make sure that
you treat your business as a real business,
and set aside funds to cover the necessary
expenses that you will need to keep the
business going.

I know that can be very hard to do when
we see those "big dollar" checks. In my early

days, I was been guilty of spending the money and didn't realize the facts until it was tax time and Uncle Sam was waiting to be paid! So make sure that you pay withholding tax payments to the IRS and state taxing authorities each quarter.

◆ Don't spend money on frivolous tech-gadgets unless you're sure that they will work for you and will save you time. Ask yourself if you really need this tool.

◆ If your marketplace has "seasonal" business (i.e., the best months are in the spring, summer, and fall), then you need to set aside money for those cold winter months when the business is not as active. Remember, you need to keep your name and your branding in front of people each and every month, or you will be wasting money.

◆ As Gary Keller says in his book *The Millionaire Real Estate Agent*, "Lead with Revenue — Not Expenses." A good rule-of-thumb is to consider that your total expenses (if you include assistants or VAs) will average about 30 percent of your gross income. This does not include the taxes that you will owe to the federal and state authorities.

Planning your life

◆ Remember to set aside some funds for fun.
◆ Remember to set aside some time for fun.

◆ When you prepare your annual goals and calendar, start with the free time that you want (and deserve). Perhaps it's a summer vacation with your family at the beach, or it might be a winter skiing vacation. Whatever it is, make sure to plan it, set aside money for it, commit to it, and stick to it.

I can recall times in my early career (and I'm sure my family remembers, too) when they were always waiting for me to finish phone calls from the hotel room so that we could all go down to the beach together. Sometimes, they gave up and left me in the room. I was too wrapped up with the old-fashioned theory that the real estate business was 24/7.

Since wisdom hopefully comes with age, I developed a new theory: "Work hard, play hard, but don't combine the two!" Today, I schedule my time much better. I don't answer phone calls at dinner time, and I don't answer cell calls immediately unless I know who is calling, and if it's a matter that needs my immediate attention.

In closing, I believe that real estate can be a very rewarding career, both in terms of self-satisfaction and monetarily. However, to make that happen, you need a passion for this business and the ability to continually focus and persevere toward your goals, while remembering that client service is our #1 priority. And, most importantly, plan to balance your time between your business and your personal life, so that you can truly enjoy the fruits of your labor!

*I hope these **18 Proven Strategies** will enhance your real estate skills...and*
My best to you for a very successful career!

TAKE ACTION!
1. Prepare your business budget and stick to it.
2. Set aside your fun time!

Appendix A

Sample "Stamp Letter" — Each time the cost of stamps increases, I buy several packets of stamps and include them with this letter to past clients.

Our 2 Cents' Worth, . . . Or, 20 of them!

The Postal Service is increasing the cost of mailing a first class letter to 41 cents on May 14th.

If you're like us, you probably have lots of 39 cent stamps . . . not many 2 cent stamps . . . and better things to do than wait in long lines at the Post Office. So, we picked up some stamps for you the other day!

Please remember to think of us, if you or anyone else you know, is considering buying or selling real estate. Everyone knows several Realtors®, but they don't know there's a big difference in *Service, Experience and Results!*

Visit us Online at
www.NewBernHomes.com

We look forward to hearing from you!
Dianne & Team

Keller Williams Realty
1915 Trent Blvd.
New Bern, NC 28560

Direct: 252-671-1932
Email: Info@NewBernHomes.com

Appendix B

Sample Halloween Mailer to past clients, sphere, and neighborhood.

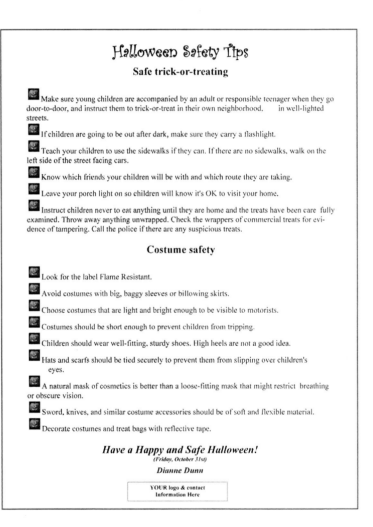

Halloween Safety Tips

Safe trick-or-treating

Make sure young children are accompanied by an adult or responsible teenager when they go door-to-door, and instruct them to trick-or-treat in their own neighborhood.   in well-lighted streets.

If children are going to be out after dark, make sure they carry a flashlight.

Teach your children to use the sidewalks if they can. If there are no sidewalks, walk on the left side of the street facing cars.

Know which friends your children will be with and which route they are taking.

Leave your porch light on so children will know it's OK to visit your home.

Instruct children never to eat anything until they are home and the treats have been care fully examined. Throw away anything unwrapped. Check the wrappers of commercial treats for evidence of tampering. Call the police if there are any suspicious treats.

Costume safety

Look for the label Flame Resistant.

Avoid costumes with big, baggy sleeves or billowing skirts.

Choose costumes that are light and bright enough to be visible to motorists.

Costumes should be short enough to prevent children from tripping.

Children should wear well-fitting, sturdy shoes. High heels are not a good idea.

Hats and scarfs should be tied securely to prevent them from slipping over children's eyes.

A natural mask of cosmetics is better than a loose-fitting mask that might restrict breathing or obscure vision.

Sword, knives, and similar costume accessories should be of soft and flexible material.

Decorate costumes and treat bags with reflective tape.

Have a Happy and Safe Halloween!
(Friday, October 31st)

Dianne Dunn

YOUR logo & contact
Information Here

The only <u>Trick</u> in Real Estate . . . is selecting the Right Realtor®!

Helping you or your friends in a real estate transaction, would be a <u>Real Treat!</u>

Just give me a call, . . .I'll Treat them Right!

Dianne Dunn

Dedicated, Knowledgeable and Responsive
to YOUR real estate needs.

Your Company Logo,
Contact info and
Website domain name HERE

Broker, CRS, GRI, e-PRO®
(Certified Internet Professional)

*Over 30 years of professional service
to Buyers and Sellers*

Please Note: If you are currently listed for sale with another broker, this is not intended as a solicitation of that listing

Appendix C

Football Magnet mailer sent to past clients, sphere, and neighborhood.

Dear Friends and Valued Clients,

It's Football Season again!

We hope that you will enjoy this magnetic schedule of the games for these PRO and College teams, with the "Monday Night" Pro schedule on the back.

(P.S. If you're not a football fan, then please pass this along to someone who would enjoy it . . . Many Thanks!)

Thank you for your business! As one of New Bern's TOP-PRODUCING Real Estate Teams, we would be happy to assist you or your friends and neighbors with *any* real estate needs.

We 💙 *Referrals!* ☺

Feel free to contact us,
The Strength of Experience = RESULTS!
Tour ALL New Bern Homes at:
www.NewBernHomes.com

KELLER WILLIAMS
1915 Trent Blvd.
New Bern, NC 28560

Direct: 252-636-3301
Toll Free: 888-781-8800
Info@NewBernHomes.com

Appendix D

Holiday e-newsletters, emailed to all past clients, sphere, leads, and neighborhood.

Ringing In St. Paddy's Day!

From Dianne Dunn
and "Team New Bern"

NewBernHomes.com
252-636-3301
888-781-8800

Spring Ahead!

Daylight Savings Time starts on March 9! Beginning in 2007, most of the United States begins Daylight Saving Time at 2:00 a.m. on the second Sunday in March and reverts to standard time on the first Sunday in November. In the U.S., each time zone switches at a different time.

Top 'o the Morn'n to ya!

We're finally into March, and looking forward to spring . . . so, regardless of your heritage, here are some web sites to help you "Ring in the Green" on St. Patrick's Day!

Tax Tips Make Filing Easier!

From Dianne Dunn
and "Team New Bern"

NewBernHomes.com
252-636-3301
888-781-8800

The lovable folks at the IRS have created The Digital Daily, a comprehensive and catchy site that includes plenty of tax information and advice, with even a handy address list of where you should file - just in case you've recently moved, or just forgotten.

The hundreds of websites won't take the sting out of signing that check over to the IRS, but they can at least give you tips on how to reduce your tax burden, list common tax errors to avoid, and what places on the web to pose tax questions.

Watch as the Tax Prophet deciphers the Internal Revenue Code for the U.S. and foreign taxpayers and professionals alike.

Most taxophobes will find helpful information in Roger A. Kahan's tax column. And for analysis, Tax Analysts can't be beat.

Samples – see page 179 for full mailer

252-636-3301
888-781-8800

KELLER WILLIAMS.

Dear Friends and Neighbors,

Unfurl the weekend! This is a time to celebrate Food, Friends and Freedom! July 4th is about our Independence on Earth, and we are very, very fortunate to have it! To learn more about this event that took place in 1776, I hope that you will peruse and enjoy some of these sites:

GOD BLESS AMERICA

"Oh, say can you see, by the dawn's early light,
What so proudly we hailed at the twilight's last gleaming?
Whose broad stripes and bright stars, through the perilous fight,
O'er the ramparts we watched, were so gallantly streaming?
And the rockets' red glare, the bombs bursting in air,
Gave proof through the night that our flag was still there.
O say, does that star-spangled banner yet wave
O'er the land of the free and the home of the brave?"

Happy Birthday America!, with patriotic music, the story of our independence, fireworks, and Mom's Apple Pie! So, let's light up the cyberworks!

Our Statue of Liberty is more important than ever! Learn about this National Monument and Ellis Island. Find out what's going on around the country this Fourth of July. Learn all about flag etiquette! And find out about past to present Fourth celebrations by clicking here!

Famous folks born on YOUR Birthday!

America's No. 1 product, far more successful than even our entertainment, space and our technology, is our love of freedom. This Fourth, I hope that when you hear The Stars and Stripes Forever, it will fill your heart with a love for our great country.

JUST FOR KIDS
★ ★ ★   ★ ★ ★

- This site covers the solar system, the universe and a variety of "space stuff" with good links to other sources.
- Take a look at NASA's photo of the earth at night with all of the lights on!
- For a history of that first flag, take a look at Betsy Ross's Home page.
- Fireworks aren't the only thing lighting our skies. For all you weather wonks, click here.
- For Safety Tips, click here.

Have a wonderful day!

Dianne

Feel free to forward this page to your family and friends, and please recommend me as your Realtor for both New and Resale Properties. Thank You!

Dianne Dunn, Broker, CRS, GRI, e-PRO®
Keller Williams® Realty
2117 South Glenburnie Rd, Suite 14
New Bern, NC 28562
(888) 781-8800 Toll Free
(252) 636-3301 Direct
Email me: DDunn@NewBernHomes.com

What's happening in Real Estate?
Click here to find out!

Search ALL New Bern Properties at:
www.SearchNewBernHomes.com

(Some of these sites have been compiled and researched by Alice Held http://www.cma2az.com)

Just For Grads!

Gifts for Grads is loaded with ideas. Find it Gift is a great internet store for computer-themed gifts.

If there was ever an online greeting card for everything and everyone, BlueMountain.com has it!

Just For Brides!

If there's someone you know taking this big step, introduce them to My Wedding Organizer, which can finalize guest lists, design seating charts, track menu selections, as well as print invitations, thank you notes, and other important documents. Get interactive Planning tools from Modern Bride.

Having a hard time thinking about what to get that happy couple? Red Envelope will give you some ideas.

Happy Thanksgiving!

NewBernHomes.com
252-636-3301
888-781-8800

From Dianne Dunn
and "Team New Bern"

Dear Neighbors and Friends,

As days get cooler and we begin to settle into our indoor activities; we realize that the Fall season is nearly drawing to a close. Our thoughts begin to turn towards the holidays with the excitement of Thanksgiving right around the corner! Before you stuff your schedule with things to do- take a minute to look at our Thanksgiving blog! From the Thanksgiving Guide for Entertainment , unbelievable Pie Recipes, the First Thanksgiving Story to fun Thanksgiving crafts for your kids and music to enjoy- you'll find this Thanksgiving Feast a perfect way to begin the holiday!

Best Wishes for a Wonderful Thanksgiving!
Dianne

Feel free to forward this page to your family and friends, and please recommend me as your Realtor for both New and Resale Properties. Thank You!

Samples – see page 183 for full mailer

About the Author

Dianne Dunn has been recognized by her peers as one of the most professional and top-producing real estate consultants for 34 years. After a successful career with IBM in their marketing support program, she began her real estate career working for a small company in Reston, Virginia in 1976, and has been affiliated with four national real estate franchise companies since then. Dianne is currently an owner/partner with Keller Williams Realty in New Bern, North Carolina, which opened in 2005.

Dianne believes in "giving back" to her real estate community through her volunteer efforts with the MLS board, and has enthusiastically embraced the technology systems and tools that will help her best serve her clients. After serving in different management and leadership roles, she enjoys teaching classes and mentoring agents in her company as well as teaching within her local association of Realtors®. Dianne has been a panelist on several Allen Hainge CyberStar™ annual summits and webinars, and more recently a CRS webinar.

Her activities in the local board included:

- Director, Neuse River Region Association 2007, 2008
- Director, New Bern MLS Service for five years, including president for two of those years.
- Chair of the Education committee for three years, as well as the Newsletter committee.

Dianne was also awarded the distinguished Realtor® of the Year Award in 2005, and the Presidential Service Award in 2004 for her extensive contributions to the MLS Service.

Dianne and her husband Lee reside in New Bern, North Carolina with their two "canine pals," Bailey and Stitch.

Index

D

database management system – 50, 51, 56, 133, 142, 153, 161
dedication – 12, 19, 20, 49, 50, 71, 107
digital camera – 153
disclosures – 91, 117, 120
domain name – 13, 151, 156

E

e-newsletter – 34, 81, 165
education – 46, 60, 63, 66, 70, 172
Excel – 17, 136, 198

F

Facebook – 155
farming – 77, 79, 80
fax-to-email – 153
Federal Housing Administration. *See* FHA
feedback – 108
FHA – 21
floor time – 72
focus – 15, 16, 20, 31, 49, 54, 55, 71, 72, 148, 165, 176
For Sale by Owner – 163
FSBO. *See* For Sale by Owner

G

goals – 8, 12, 46, 49, 50, 53, 54, 56, 59, 60, 70, 158, 176
Godin, Seth – 17
Going Green – 66, 147
Good Faith Estimate – 92
Google – 107
Graduate of the Real Estate Institute, GRI® – 65

H

Hainge, Allen – 152
Held, Alice – 34
Homes Magazine – 136

I

incentive – 108, 110, 111, 171
Inman News – 68
inspections – 101
Internet – 13, 26, 52, 66, 77, 87, 107, 135, 136, 143, 145, 148, 154, 169, 173
Internet marketing – 26, 77, 135, 136, 143, 145

J

K
Keller, Gary – 59
Keller Williams Realty – 59, 189

L
laptop computer– 153
lead generation – 50, 52, 78, 160, 164
lender's letter – 89
local content – 145, 156

M
manual – 20, 158, 162–164, 170–172
marketing – 13, 19, 26, 46, 63, 77, 79, 80, 82, 105, 107, 108, 111, 115, 121,
    127, 128, 135, 136, 143, 145, 154, 158, 173, 189
McDonnell, Leslie – 35
mentor/mentoring – 12, 16, 17, 69, 131, 189
mindset – 15, 50
MLS – 32, 33, 46, 48, 55, 68, 73, 80, 81, 99, 105, 106, 119, 120, 146, 151,
    160, 174, 189, 190
Monroe, Zan – 33
Multiple Listing Service. – *See* MLS
Multiple offers – 121

N
NAR® – 24, 26, 64
National Association of Realtors®. *See* NAR®
negotiation/negotiating – 13, 127, 128, 130
No Risk, No Reward – 128

O
open houses – 72, 74, 75, 87, 136, 160

P
Pareto Principle. *See* 80/20 Rule
pipeline – 71
PMA – 12, 41, 42, 43
positive attitude – 20, 43
Positive Mental Attitude. *See* PMA
postcard – 82, 85
pre-approval – 89
Pre-Listing Package – 105, 116

U

V

W

X-Y-Z

Forms and Templates

All of the forms and templates in *Top 18 Proven Stategies for a Successful Career in Real Estate* are available for purchase online at:

www.SuccessfulRealEstateTips.com

The forms and templates are available in MS Word and MS Excel formats, and are editable to suit your specific needs. On this site you can also order additional copies of the book.

9 780982 629352